3000 800059 69648
St. Louis Community College

Florissant Valley Library
St. Louis Community College
3400 Pershall Road
Ferguson, MO 63135-1499
314-595-4514

D0072971

THE BOOK

THE BOOK

THE LIFE STORY
OF A TECHNOLOGY

Nicole Howard

GREENWOOD TECHNOGRAPHIES

GREENWOOD PRESS
Westport, Connecticut • London

Library of Congress Cataloging-in-Publication Data

Howard, Nicole.
   The book : the life story of a technology / Nicole Howard.
      p. cm.—(Greenwood technographies, ISSN 1549-7321)
   Includes bibliographical references and index.
   ISBN 0–313–33028–X (alk. paper)
      1. Books—History. 2. Printing—History. I. Title. II. Series.
   Z4.H69   2005
   002' .09—dc22   2005013436

British Library Cataloguing in Publication Data is available.

Copyright © 2005 by Nicole Howard

All rights reserved. No portion of this book may be
reproduced, by any process or technique, without the
express written consent of the publisher.

Library of Congress Catalog Card Number: 2005013436
ISBN: 0–313–33028–X
ISSN: 1549–7321

First published in 2005

Greenwood Press, 88 Post Road West, Westport, CT 06881
An imprint of Greenwood Publishing Group, Inc.
www.greenwood.com

Printed in the United States of America

The paper used in this book complies with the
Permanent Paper Standard issued by the National
Information Standards Organization (Z39.48–1984).

10 9 8 7 6 5 4 3 2 1

Contents

Series Foreword

In today's world, technology plays an integral role in the daily life of people of all ages. It affects where we live, how we work, how we interact with each other, and what we aspire to accomplish. To help students and the general public better understand how technology and society interact, Greenwood has developed *Greenwood Technographies*, a series of short, accessible books that trace the histories of these technologies while documenting *how* these technologies have become so vital to our lives.

Each volume of the *Greenwood Technographies* series tells the biography or "life story" of a particularly important technology. Each life story traces the technology from its "ancestors" (or antecedent technologies), through its early years (either its invention or development) and rise to prominence, to its final decline, obsolescence, or ubiquity. Just as a good biography combines an analysis of an individual's personal life with a description of the subject's impact on the broader world, each volume in the *Greenwood Technographies* series combines a discussion of technical developments with a description of the technology's effect on the broader fabric of society and culture—and vice versa. The technologies covered in the series run the gamut from those that have been around for centuries—firearms and the printed book, for example—to recent inventions that have rapidly taken over the modern world, such as electronics and the computer.

While the emphasis is on a factual discussion of the development of the technology, these books are also fun to read. The history of technology is full of fascinating tales that both entertain and illuminate. The authors—all experts in their fields—make the life story of technology come alive, while also providing readers with a profound understanding of the relationship of science, technology, and society.

Introduction

For books are not absolutely dead things, but do contain a potency of life in them to be active as that soul whose progeny they are; nay, they do preserve as in a vial the purest efficacy and extraction of that living intellect that bred them . . .

—John Milton, 1643 address to Parliament

This volume is one in a series of biographies of technologies. They trace the adolescences and adulthoods of technologies as various as airplanes, automobiles, computer chips, and X rays. From their infancy—rudimentary devices in the hands of their creators—through their maturation into full-fledged adult technologies, the life stories of these innovations unfold with surprising complexity. As with a person's biography, the biography of a technology is not limited to the object alone, but must encompass the history of people, places, and ideas that gave rise to the innovation. This biography of the book will do just that.

The life in question here—the life of a book—is one that may not immediately strike a parallel with more familiar technologies. Hundreds of pages sewn together, bearing printed or handwritten material, hardly compares to supersonic jets and Pentium chips. But in fact, no other technology in human history has had the impact of this invention. Indeed, the book is the one technology that has made all the others possible, by recording and storing information and ideas indefinitely in a convenient and readily accessible place. Books represent a peak of technology, giving permanence and form to ideas and knowledge.

WHAT COUNTS AS TECHNOLOGY?

In the twenty-first century, we are surrounded by technologies that have affected our lives on a grand scale, but that are widely different from each other: biotechnology and information technology. These are wholly different species and they exemplify the problem of clearly identifying what constitutes a technology. Scholars debate this question regularly, but most agree that technology—from the Greek word *technē*, meaning craft or skill—is a man-made artifact that serves a practical function. Technology is understood to be distinct from pure science; in fact, it represents the application and manifestation of scientific ideas in some useful, material form.

Among the most common of technological artifacts today are those related to the preservation and transfer of data, be they PDAs, cell phones, or televisions. Preceding all of these, however, is the book: the single greatest example of information technology of the second millenium. On its pages, the book presents both text and images—culturally understood representations of knowledge that are being preserved and transferred.

In an oral culture, the closest equivalent to the book was memory. People exchanged stories and ideas with each other, each time altering the product slightly as they recollected it. But with the introduction of systems of writing (around 6000 B.C.E.), the products of memory could be fixed in images and words. The convenience of writing systems was further enhanced by collecting them in new ways: on tablets, scrolls, or wooden boards. The book was an outgrowth of these developments, an artifact that sits at the center of multiple related technologies.

To tell the story of how books originated and grew into their present form requires us to consider a broad subset of technologies: the creation of illustrations, the mixing of inks, the preparation of parchment, the making of paper, the casting of type, and the engineering of print, among other activities. The sciences involved in these processes range from metallurgy to chemistry to mechanics. Taken together, they form a web of technologies that culminate in the book.

This history examines the evolution of books: their life story from early papyrus scrolls—which hardly seem like books at first glance—to modern paperbacks. And any good biography engages in genealogy, exploring the family tree to discover limbs and branches of distant relatives. The history of books is no different. The generations of ancestral records that lead up to the modern book reveal a dynamic series of technological innovations. Their progeny is the book you hold in your hand. By examining the book as a technology, we get the best example of how profoundly information and media technology affect culture and history, and how vital the technology of the book has been to cultural and intellectual change.

Timeline

2600 B.C.E.	Papyrus used as a writing surface.
100 C.E.	Approximate appearance of the first codex.
105	Ts'ai Lun proposes the idea of paper to China's Han emperor.
300–400	Parchment began replacing papyrus as a preferred writing surface.
300–800	*Uncial* script commonly used by scribes.
ca. 750	Chinese prisoners build first paper mill in Samarkand for Muslim captors.
Late eighth century	Caroline minuscule script developed by Alcuin of York for Charlemagne.
800	Paper introduced in Baghdad from the East.
Eleventh century	Chinese develop a moveable type for printing, from baked clay.
1074	First European paper mill established in eastern Spain by Muslims.
Twelfth century	Gothic script introduced, also known as "Textur" or "Black Letter."
1270	Paper mill established near Rome.

Fourteenth century	"Humanist" script developed by Renaissance scholars.
1399	Johannes Gutenberg born in Mainz, in today's Germany.
1456	A printed Bible attributed to Gutenberg is issued from Mainz.
1457	Johann Fust and Peter Schöffer print the *Mainz Psalter.*
1460	The *Mainz Catholicon* is printed, also attributed to Gutenberg.
1493	Anton Koberger publishes the *Nuremberg Chronicle.*
1498	Albrecht Dürer's *Apocalypse* series is published.
1455–1500	Period of *Incunables*, books printed in the fifteenth century.
1522	Martin Luther's German Bible is issued from a Wittenberg press.
1539	Juan de Zumárraga establishes a printing press and paper mill in Spanish-controlled Mexico.
1555	Christophe Plantin establishes a printing house in Antwerp.
1557	London Stationer's Company is formed with royal charter to monitor publication of books.
1580	Louis Elzevier settles in Leiden; opens first Elzevier print house. By 1638 the Elzeviers are producing books in The Hague, Amsterdam, and Utrecht.
1638	Mrs. Jose Glover establishes first printing press in British North America.
1662	Licensing Act (or Press Act) is passed in England to increase royal control on published books. Expired in 1695.
1710	England's Copyright Act is enacted, recognizing authorial rights.
1730	Benjamin Franklin becomes official printer to the state of Pennsylvania.
1751	Diderot begins publication of the *Encyclopédie*, completed in 1772.
1798	Nicolas Louis Robert automates paper production with his Endless Wire Papermaking Machine.
1798	Alois Senefelder develops lithography, or "stone printing."
1801	A papermaking machine, known as the Fourdrinier, is patented in England.
1803	Charles Stanhope, third Earl Stanhope, builds the first iron press. Manufactured in New York in 1811 and Germany in 1815.

1804   Charles Stanhope develops stereotyping method.

1810   Fredrich König's first steam-powered press is patented in England.

1813   George Clymer develops the "Columbian," first handpress built in America made from iron.

1814   König's single-cylinder, web-fed, steam-powered press is used to print *The Times* of London.

1816   Cylindrical stereotyping plates introduced for use with rotary presses.

1822   Richard Cope introduces the "Albion" press, with improved toggle system to replace the screw mechanism of earlier presses.

1826   König's press is adapted for the mass production of books.

1830   Isaac Adams patents the Adams power press, the most commonly used platen press in America at the time.

1834   The London Union Company of Compositors forms to protect trade threatened by automation.

1838   David Bruce invents a machine that creates type automatically.

1839   Fox Talbot introduces photography.

1839   Electrotyping introduced, allowing print through electroplating.

1843   Friedrich Gottlob Keller replaces rag pulp with wood pulp in papermaking.

1844   Fox Talbot's *The Pencil of Nature* is published, the first work to include photographs.

1846   Richard Hoe develops the Hoe Type-Revolving Machine, which prints not from a bed of type, but type wrapped around a cylinder.

1851   First lithographic power press introduced.

1861   Two-colored printing is introduced on a single-cylinder press.

1863   William Bullock combines a papermaking machine with the type-revolving press to produce a web-fed, perfecting, power printer.

1879   David M. Smyth patents a machine to sew book bindings.

1879   Photogravure is introduced by Karl Klič.

1885   Linn Boyd Benton patents the Pantograph, a mechanical engraver that creates both punches and matrices.

1886   Ottmar Mergenthaler develops the Linotype machine, automating both typecasting and composition.

1891   William Morris's fine-art Kelmscott Press is started.

1896   Tolbert Lanston receives a patent for his Monotype machine.

1903   Ira Rubel develops offset printing, a lithographic technique involving three cylinders, which quickly becomes the industry standard.

1908   Aniline printing is developed, but not commonly used until the 1950s when it was renamed flexographic printing.

1935   Penguin Books is established by Sir Allen Lane, and becomes a major publisher in the "paperback revolution" of the early twentieth century.

1937   Xerography introduced by Chester Carlson.

1939   Pocket Books is founded in the United States, becoming a major paperback publisher.

1950   The first photocompositor, Intertype Fotosetter, is built.

1953   The first book printed with photocomposition appears.

1971   Project Gutenberg begins converting book to electronic format.

1990   Xerox introduces DocuTech, which automates book production and allows for small, affordable print runs.

2001   E-ink and e-paper are developed, technologies that promise to alter the fundamental materials used in making books.

1

Ancestors: Books before Print

THE GENERATIONS BEFORE PRINT

The life story of books is an exploration not only of the physical evolution of the book, but its development as a cultural artifact. The very book you read from now has such an extensive and rich history that we must go back thousands of years to find its earliest ancestors. In doing so, we discover writing on surfaces that are nothing like paper, gathered together in formats hardly resembling books, and read by select groups of people far smaller than today's general readership. Nevertheless, these ancestral forms of the book were treated in familiar ways: they were read aloud, collected by wealthy individuals, loaned from libraries, stacked up in university class-rooms, exchanged among friends, given as gifts, and sold in bookstores. As we chronicle the earliest generations of books on the family tree, we can appreciate these activities, even if the physical form of such early books was quite different from today's.

Books act both as physical objects—something constructed from any variety of materials—and as preservers and conduits of information. They have been poetically dedicated and generously decorated, praised and criticized, and even banned and burned as representations of ideas that are unacceptable in a given time and place. Thus, the history of their construction and the story of their dissemination into the wider culture is one worth exploring.

This chapter begins the exploration by considering the ancestors to the modern book: those created prior to the introduction of the printing press in the fifteenth century.

Long before Johannes Gutenberg set up his printing shop in Germany, books were being made around the globe. Naturally, different cultures approached the task of recording ideas in unique ways: some used alphabets, others relied wholly on images, and still others employed such items as knotted strings to record information. Our notion of what constitutes a book must be broad enough to encompass such diverse cultural efforts, and it must take into account the fact that numerous intercultural encounters over time led to cross-fertilization, so that ideas about books were both shared and rapidly spread.

Our survey begins with the generations of books that developed between antiquity (around 800 B.C.E.) and the European Renaissance of the fourteenth century. The bookmaking tradition that we will focus on is centered in Europe, but its heritage can be definitively linked to technologies from the Far East, especially China. Thus, the early history of books is necessarily a history of the transmission and adoption of an array of Chinese, Korean, and Japanese techniques for recording information and images. It is also a study of the unique approaches different cultures have brought to constructing books.

From clay tablets in Sumeria to Moabite stone in Phoenicia, the "hardware" of books has varied widely. Likewise, the appearance of the written word and image has been adapted to suit the practical constraints of a book. Writing varies depending on the kind of information being preserved, the nature of the surface on which it appears, and the kind of writing or imprinting device employed. Studying the many differences among early books allows us to better appreciate the artifact in its modern form, while at the same time shedding light on its evolution. This chapter begins with an examination of scrolls and tablets, which can seem like historical novelties to the modern reader. It ends in the fourteenth century, when handwritten books made their appearance in a structure we would recognize today as not unlike our own books.

Writing Surfaces: Papyrus to Parchment

Words, pictures, and symbols have been inscribed on a multitude of surfaces in what can be considered the ancient relatives of books. In 3000 B.C.E., Hammurabi, who conquered much of Mesopotamia, issued a code of 282 laws that was recorded on a piece of stone known as a "stele." Preserved for millennia, the writing on this stone has offered scholars important insight into this ancient civilization. Likewise, the Assyrians, a western Asian people who thrived in the seventh and eighth centuries B.C.E., recorded information and events on clay tablets, pieces of wood, and bone. Other known writing surfaces of the ancient world include ivory, tortoise shell, linen, bast fiber (a woody fiber from certain plants), and palm leaves. Whatever would hold an impression was used, and while a clay cylinder with cuneiform writing on it is not what we would consider a book, it certainly counts among the ancestors of book technology. The shape would change and the materials would evolve, but there is a clear link between wooden tablets etched with a shell and today's hardback books.

For a more recognizable ancestor to the printed book, one needs to go back several thousand years to northern Africa. As early as 2600 B.C.E., records were kept by Egyptians on papyrus, a plant that grew in abundance along the banks of the Nile River in Egypt. The process of turning these reeds into paper was described in detail by Pliny the Elder, in the thirteenth chapter of his famous *Natural History*, written in the first century C.E.

First, the stalks of papyrus plants were cut into 2-foot segments and the rind removed. Inside was a pulp-like substance, or pith, made largely of cellulose. This pith was removed and then flattened out into strips, which were lined up next to each other so that the edges touched. A second layer of pithy strips was then placed perpendicularly on top of the first, and the two layers glued together with a starchy substance. Pliny indicated that this glue came from the waters of the Nile itself, but historians are doubtful. More likely, the liquid sap from the reed acted as a glue between the layers. The crosswise placement of the papyrus strips made for a stronger surface, though it had the disadvantage of rendering one side—where the papyrus ran vertically—useless for writing. The horizontal side, however, was easily written upon, the strips acting like lines on modern notebook paper.

Once the layers of papyrus were arranged in this crisscross fashion, they were placed in a press or else hammered together. When dry, they proved to be both flexible and durable, enough so that they could be written upon without breaking apart. Though the papyrus sheets were not much more than twelve inches in height, they could be glued to each other to create very long writing surfaces, some fifty to one hundred feet long. By any measure this is a cumbersome length to manage as a reader, and ultimately, scrolls were divided up into tomes (from the Greek word *tomos*, meaning "to cut") to make them more manageable. A single author could then write a work that was divided among several scrolls.

Pliny described nine different types of papyrus, revealing incredible variation in the writing surface. Among these types, the "Regia" papyrus was the largest papyrus sheet made, while the "Livia" shared the "Regia" dimensions but provided a thinner sheet. "Hieratica" papyri were valued for their whiteness, which priests preferred, and "Charta Claudia" (named for Emperor Claudius) offered a sheet durable and thick enough to take writing on both sides, though archaeologists have found that the practice of writing on two sides was uncommon. "Emporetic" served as a kind of wrapping paper, and "Taeniotica"—sold by weight rather than by the sheet—was a commonly used type of papyrus made in Alexandria (Vitale 1971, 108).

To write on these rolls of papyrus, Egyptians used reeds or soft quills, which were cut at the end to form pointed tips. A common reed of this type was called a *calamus* and, dipped in an ink made from charcoal and water, served as a pen. The scribe would write in sections on the papyrus, wait for it to dry, and then continue his work. Histories, works of literature, poems, music, and civic records were recorded by Egyptians in this way. Scrolls were also copied regularly by scribes, who would either transcribe directly from one scroll to another, or else write down what was read to them aloud. It was a slow and painstaking process.

Today, numerous papyrus scrolls from ancient Egypt are extant, thanks to their durability. Among these are the Abbott Papyrus, a legal text kept in the British Museum; the Ebers Papyrus, a medical text; the Prisse Papyrus, a moral text housed in France's Bibliothèque Nationale, and the Rhind Papyrus, a mathematical work.

Papyrus served the needs of ancient writers for centuries. But the increasing use of parchment (untanned leather) in the first century C.E. marked a turning point in the history of books. Leather became an increasingly common writing surface as papyrus grew scarce. The reasons for this scarcity are a source of debate. According to many historians, a shortage of the papyrus reed along the Nile River led Egyptians to limit their exports. Just as likely is the explanation that a series of attacks on Egypt in the second century B.C.E. drastically lowered their ability to supply the reed to neighboring regions. One area affected by this supply problem was Pergamum, a kingdom in ancient Mysia, known today as Bergama, Turkey. In response to the shortage, King Eumenes II (r. 197–159 B.C.E.) ordered his officials to utilize an alternative writing surface, and their answer was parchment or, as it was called, "Charta Pergamena."

Parchment, which technically refers to the softened and untanned skins of sheep, and vellum—the term for calfskin—both proved better substrates than papyrus for several reasons. First, they could be made anywhere there were animals, eliminating the regional dependency on Egypt's reeds, which proved costly when supplies were low. Second, parchment and vellum were much more durable and would outlast papyrus by hundreds of years. Third, when properly treated, untanned leather offered a much better writing surface than papyrus.

To make parchment, the animal skin was cleaned and scraped to remove hair and as much of the dirt as possible. It was then treated with lime and pumice, which both cleaned the surface and closed the pores, making it smoother. Finally, it was dried and cut to the appropriate size for writing. All told, creating parchment for writing purposes was a difficult task, since the skins had to be both stretched and dried at the same time. The skin that is ultimately written upon has been, essentially, dried out in an expanded position, never to retract.

The hard work that went into parchment creation paid off. Not only was it a strong and flexible material, but writing looked much sharper on parchment than it had on papyrus. Moreover, it had the distinct advantage of allowing erasures. It was also possible to write on both sides of the sheet because the ink did not bleed through, and there were no awkward ridges to prevent it, as there had been with vertically oriented papyrus leaves. Though papyrus was still used in the first few centuries C.E., it had—by the fourth century—been almost completely replaced with parchment. Scribes of the early Christian Church began transferring material from the papyrus rolls to parchment so that it could be more easily read, stored, and preserved.

Introduction of Paper

While papyrus and parchment were being used in the West, the Chinese developed the craft of making paper, which, they quickly realized, was a cheap and useful writing surface. Credit is usually given to Ts'ai Lun, an official in the court of Han emperor Han Ho Ti, who proposed the idea in 105 C.E. More recently, however, historians and archeologists have pushed back the date of paper's first appearance to sometime between 140 and 86 B.C.E.

Initially the Chinese used silk cloth to make paper, but the expense quickly prompted a search for a more affordable alternative. Silk was first replaced with hemp, which was broken down into small fibers. But the hemp was eventually replaced with a combination of bark, scraps of rags that had been discarded, and bast fiber. Making a smooth sheet of paper from these coarse substances required a long initial soaking. The rags, bark, and other scraps were left in a bin of water until they began to break down, forming a kind of paste. This paste was then stirred and pressed to remove the water. When this fibrous mixture dried the result was a crude form of paper. Initially, it was rougher on the surface than scribes preferred, but ways of smoothing it out were developed. The paper proved durable and efficient.

Around the sixth century C.E., papermaking techniques developed in China were adopted in Korea, and from there were introduced in Japan by a Korean monk. It was not until the eighth century, when Chinese papermakers were taken captive by Arab armies in Samarkand (in present-day Uzbekistan), that papermaking techniques began to move westward. The migration of this technology was facilitated both by the presence of the "Silk Road," an established trade route that linked China to the Mediterranean, and by the expansion of the Arab Empire—which coalesced after the death of the Prophet, Muhammad. The spread of Muslim culture and values is especially important in the history of books.

Under the Muslim leaders, known as "caliphs," the Umayyad dynasty spread both the Arabic language and Islamic beliefs to much of the known world between 660 and 750 C.E. With its capital in Damascus, the empire expanded westward into northern Africa and Spain, and eastward into central Asia. Thus, the empire acted as a middleman, facilitating the exchange of knowledge and goods between China, India, Persia (present-day Iran), and Byzantium. Among the technologies that were transferred to the West through the rich cross-fertilization efforts of the Muslims was the Chinese technique of making paper. But instead of using silk, which was not in great supply in the West, Arab craftsmen made paper from linen rags and vegetable fibers. By the ninth century, paper was being used extensively by their administrators and bureaucrats throughout the empire, whose record keeping was integral to the success of the dynasty.

When the Umayyad Empire declined in the eighth century, the new caliph established the Abbasid Empire, with its capital in Baghdad. The Abbasids ruled from 750 to 1258 C.E. and contributed even further to the developed book technologies. In 832, the *Bayt al Hikma*, or "House of Wisdom" was built in Baghdad as a center for book production, textual translation, and scholarship. The House of Wisdom included a library, astronomical observatory, and a collection of scrolls from ancient Greece that Muslim scholars had retrieved for the purpose of copying and studying. Baghdad was, for a time, the intellectual center of the world. Moreover, as scribes increasingly used paper in books, copies became more affordable, so that even middle-class citizens in major cities could afford to buy books.

The importance of books was not limited to the Abbasid capital, but spread throughout the empire. Thus, in the Spanish city of Cordoba, under Muslim control, yet another major library was established. There, amid 400,000 books, scribes, illuminators, and bookbinders created beautiful reproductions of ancient texts. Cordoban leather, famous today for its high quality, was first used by Muslim binders, who covered their books' wooden boards with treated horse hides.

Unfortunately, the highly-skilled craftsmen of Cordoba's library were forced out in the thirteenth century by European crusaders who successfully wrested the city from the Muslims. In the process, they sacked many of the buildings. Much of Cordoba's library was lost, but fortunately for Europe (and for this history), the bookmaking technology that the Muslims introduced to Spain did not disappear with the library. Indeed, in other Iberian cities the techniques introduced by Arabs were being practiced, and a healthy book culture endured.

The Spanish cities of Toledo and Valencia both had paper mills operating in the twelfth century, and by 1276 there was a mill in Italy and another was established in Nuremberg in 1390. Ultimately, paper would replace vellum throughout western Europe as the material of choice for producing books, principally because its manufacture was easier and cheaper than that of parchment.

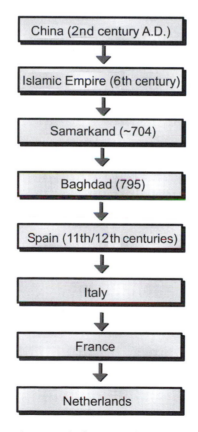

The spread of papermaking technology from China to the West.

The process of making paper had scarcely changed over the thousand years it took to reach western Europe. Typically, European paper mills made pulp from scraps of cotton and linen, but at times even old fishing nets or other fibrous scraps were included. The mix of linen—called half-stuff—was left in a pot of water to ferment and decompose. After the material started to break down, the mushy substance was boiled and then rinsed with fresh water to remove any dirt or residue. The watery pulp solution that remained after rinsing was agitated with beaters, causing the fibers to further decompose, and then poured into a large vat. If the process was started with 100 pounds of rags, there would be, after pulping, approximately 88 pounds of pulp, the extra material being lost in the processing.

For paper of a very high quality, a few extra steps were required, causing additional expense. First, the rags used to make pulp had to come from high-quality materials, such as silk. The rags would also be cut by hand, rather than by a machine that was commonly used. Finally, the half-stuff would be washed before it was turned into pulp, and the pulp rinsed an extra time, all in an effort to eliminate residue. Few paper mills, however, went to such lengths.

The key to making any paper from pulp was the extraction of the tiny fibers from the half-stuff (the watery, pulpy mixture), and to do this, a special frame was dipped into the vat of pulp. Though seemingly straightforward, it took an experienced vatman to carry out this task. When he dipped the frame into the vat, he ensured that the wet fibers adhered in just the right way. Too many fibers and the paper would not dry properly; too few and the sheet of paper was worthless. The frame he used had wires running across it like a sieve or a screen, so that the fibers readily stuck to it. In some cases, a printing house would make a design out of wire, which sat in the middle of the frame. This design was called a watermark.

Once the vatman was sure that the pulp had properly adhered to the frame, he removed and handed it to an assistant who scraped off the excess water with felt pads. This was a delicate process because the wet fibers were easily moved and ruined. When the paper had dried enough on the screen to allow it to be moved, it was placed on a piece of felt. As the sheets of paper dried, they were stacked up, still separated by felt to prevent sticking. Once 144 sheets were stacked up, they were placed beneath a press so that the last bits of water could be squeezed out of them. A stack of paper (interspersed with felt) that was 2 feet thick was quickly reduced to 6 inches beneath the force of the press. The felts were removed, a second, less forceful press was applied, and then the sheets were stacked again to dry. The pressing had a double function: it removed water from the paper and also smoothed out the surface, making it better for writing. Sometimes paper was treated an additional time with a glutinous substance and then rubbed with a glossy stone to give it an even smoother surface. The tiny pores of

Woodcut of a vatman making paper, by Jost Amman, 1568. This item is reproduced by permission of The Huntington Library, San Marino, California.

the paper were sealed up by the rubbing of the stone, so that when the pen tip hit the paper, the ink would not spread out through the individual fibers nearly as much. All that remained once the paper was dried and smoothed was to cut it to an appropriate size.

Initial resistance to papermaking in Europe can be attributed in part to paper's connection with the Islamic world. In 1221, the Holy Roman Emperor Frederick II issued a decree that invalidated any government documents written on paper, such a Muslim tool being unwelcomed in Christendom. But the sanction was hardly effective. Paper mills quickly spread throughout Europe, and as mills became more efficient, costs dropped, in the fifteenth century, to the point where paper was one-sixth the price of vellum.

ANCESTRAL APPEARANCES: FROM SCROLL TO CODEX

Initially, papyrus and parchment were kept as scrolls that could be unrolled either vertically or horizontally, depending on the direction of the script. The horizontal form was more common, and because scrolls could be quite long, a scribe would typically refrain from writing a single line across the entire length, but instead would mark off columns of a reasonable width. That way the reader could unroll one side and roll up the other while reading. Nevertheless, the constant need to re-roll the scroll was a major disadvantage to this format, and it was impossible to jump to various places in the scroll the way we skip to a particular page of a book. Moreover, the reader struggled to make notes while reading since both hands (or weights) were required to keep the scroll open. We take for granted the ease with which we can write or type as we read. In the era of scrolls the scholar's hands were often tethered to his reading material.

Once they were stored, there was the added problem of telling scrolls apart. Titles of today's books are on the spine, and therefore quickly read, but that innovation did not appear until there were books such as we have today, with actual spines. Readers of scrolls dealt with the problem of identification by applying small tags to the upper edges of scrolls. In Greek these were called *sillybos* (from whence we derive the term syllabus), while the Romans referred to them as *titlus* (from whence we get the term title). The tags made it easier to organize and identify scrolls, but there remained the problem of storage. Being rounded, they did not lend themselves to neat stacking. Instead, scrolls were placed in groups in a stone or wooden jar, known in Greek as a *bibliotheke*. Those who have studied a Romance language—such as Spanish—will recognize this as the word used today for "library." Thus, the earliest libraries stored tubular books according to their topics.

Though most papyrus was rolled in the traditional way, there were some instances when it was folded back and forth upon itself, similar to the way in which maps are folded today. The same folding technique was occasionally applied to parchment as well, which resulted in an accordion-like series of creases that could be unfolded and refolded while reading. This seemingly minor transition—the switch from rolling to folding—signaled a key step toward a more user-friendly book, since folding allowed the reader to skip ahead in the material more easily. There are also a few known examples of papyrus sheets that were stacked up and then sewn together on one side, though books of this form are the exception rather than the rule.

The replacement of papyrus with parchment, and the switch from scrolls to folded pages, both marked major changes in the appearance and utility of ancient books. Following on the heels of these innovations was another significant alteration, one that ushered in the truly modern form of the book. This was the codex.

Beginning in the first century C.E., a small tablet-like tool, known as a diptych, was used by the Romans to record information. Consisting of two panels, the diptych was a folding tablet made from boards, often ebony or boxwood, that were hinged together on one side with string or leather straps. Imagine the cover of a book with no pages inside, and you have some idea of what these tools looked like. The two outer faces were covered in leather and decorated with jewels or a royal emblem, and the two inner faces were coated with wax. One could use a stylus or some other sharp-edged implement to write directly on the wax. When the information was no longer needed, it could simply be erased, or rubbed out, and the surface reused.

Although there were no parchment sheets in a diptych, their structural potential was quickly realized. It was not long before the Romans were applying this format to gatherings of parchment or papyrus in a format called a codex. Codices (plural) consisted of "a collection of sheets of any material, folded double and fastened together at the back or the spine, and usually protected by covers" (Roberts and Skeat 1983, 1). The codex format, however, was slow to be adopted. Though scholars have dated the oldest extant parchment codex (written in Latin) to 100 C.E., historical record clearly shows that the Romans continued to rely on scrolls into the third century. The Roman writer Martial (38–104 C.E.) was the first scholar to mention the existence of a parchment codex in his writings, where he commented on the portability of the format. Not until the fifth century did codices become truly commonplace, and even then, such notable figures as Saints Augustine and Jerome were using scrolls in their private correspondence.

The codex remained in use through the early days of the Christian Church, with scribes in Rome and throughout Latin Christendom copying religious works and securing them between the elaborately decorated wooden boards. As religious symbols, these books were prized, and their beauty was such that they would sometimes adorn the altar. Inside, the handwriting and illustrations equaled the exterior, displaying painstaking attention to detail. Among the branches of the church, it was the Benedictine monks who seemed to reflect their reverence for books with the greatest enthusiasm. Their libraries were numbered among the greatest collections of texts of the time, and their scribes and craftsmen masterfully coupled the art and technology of bookmaking.

Making a Medieval Book

Assume for a moment that you are a monk in a fourteenth-century monastery and you have been ordered to prepare a blank book for a scribe, who will copy a work into it. Your task requires more than simply ordering a piece of parchment. First, you would need to determine the appropriate size for the parchment sheets, which would depend on what kind of book the scribe had in mind. Was it about herbs, with pages large enough to accommodate full-size illustrations of local plants? Or was it a section of the Old Testament, in which case the pages might need to be smaller for the sake of portability? Perhaps it was a songbook, to be used for the music during mass. These questions would need to be answered before the parchment or vellum was cut.

Typically, the entire skin of a young calf was needed for each piece of vellum. Once treated so that it was fit for writing, the edges had to be trimmed, and the sheets folded down the middle. This created what is called a folio: a sheet of paper folded in half one time. The folded half is referred to as a leaf of parchment (or vellum), and once folded, you end up with four usable pages: the front and back of each half. Next, the folios had to be grouped together, with four to five of them nested inside each other to form a series of minibooklets. The final step was to tie these booklets together with string, using good knots that are neither too bulky nor too loose. There were various ways of stitching the pages together, but the result was a series of fresh parchment pages bound to each other in what resembled a book without a cover. Your task would now be through and this blank book sent on to the scribe.

With their sheets of parchment books prepared, scribes began months, if not years, of work, copying a text word for word. Their work took place in a room of the monastery called the *scriptorium*, literally, "the writing room," devoted solely to the copying of books. Typically, several scribes collaborated on a given book—each doing a different part—in order to

A scribe at work copying a manuscript. Courtesy of the Library of Congress.

expedite the copying. In this way, a book could be produced in as little as a month.

Many of the books copied in this period were duplications of works that had long existed, such as the Old and New Testament, and famous scriptural commentaries by church leaders. Despite the popularity of these works, relatively few copies were in circulation; therefore, monasteries frequently shared books from their libraries with one another so that copies could be made and added to the existing collections. Both the tedium of copying and the exactitude with which scribes had to write, made this difficult work.

Adding to the labor of the copyist were the efforts of the illuminator. Illuminators were artists who, using bold pigments, decorated manuscript books with a variety of pictures and ornamentations, particularly in the margins and around capital letters. Most medieval works were liturgical in nature, and thus, illuminations tended to treat religious themes. Scholars estimate that one out of forty manuscripts in the Middle Ages had some kind of illumination, whether it was a decorated capital letter, an ornate border around the page, or miniature pictures that were placed alongside the text (Griffiths and Pearsall 1989, 31). These were almost always added to the page after the text was written, and were traditionally of bright colors or gold.

Like the scribes who carefully copied a work in a specific hand, illuminators were highly-skilled men. They typically worked in a separate room from scribes where their tools and dyes were readily available. In some instances, illuminators were not part of the clergy, but offered their skills to the monastery for a period of time. In such cases, the rules required that "if there are craftsmen in the monastery they should pursue their crafts with all humility after the abbot has given permission" (Alexander 1992, 5). Their craft involved decorating the capital letters and artistically filling in much of the white space on the page, often with allegorical illustrations. When they were finished, the result was a prized possession, a book treated with the utmost care and delicacy. And yet, despite the brilliance of many medieval illuminations, very few of the illuminators are known since their names were not recorded.

Sewing the folios together effectively kept the pages connected, but there was still the problem of protecting the book once it was finished, as well as preventing wear on the outer edges. The unbound pages of a finished book—including any leaves added at the front or back—are known as the bookblock. This bookblock was tied with linked sewing, a strong stitch that, when doubled up, kept the pages firmly in place. The stitching along the edge of the pages formed the spine, which was then covered in parchment. Finally, the book was covered in wooden boards, literally turning it into a hardback.

Typically, the boards would be covered with vellum or parchment wrapped around the spine of the book. In addition to making the wooden cover look better, the leather protected the stitches holding the pages together. In some cases, scrapped parchment was pasted together to form a thick covering, almost like cardboard, and this could be covered with leather and used to bind a book. It was not nearly as sturdy as wood, but if made with sufficient plies it proved as effective as a binding.

However, the book's front (opposite the spine) remained exposed and susceptible to wear. And the parchment sheets had a tendency to curl up unless pressure was kept on it. To prevent this, the boards were made to extend beyond the pages and were hooked together with clasps, sometimes with a small lock on them. With the boards held firmly together, the parchment was forced to remain flat and was protected from wear and tear.

Both the clasps and the leather covering presented opportunities to decorate the book. For nicer volumes, produced for wealthier monasteries or patrons, floral designs, crests, and religious scenes could be engraved or impressed onto the leather cover—the latter process known as blind tooling. The process was similar to branding, though the design of the stamp was engraved on either metal or wood. The earliest blind-tooled book dates from the thirteenth century, and the practice became increasingly common thereafter, especially in the Netherlands. In addition to the stamping, which could be made to cover the entire cover of a book, ornamental metal knobs, known as "bosses," were used. These protruded from the front cover in the same way gems would.

Another common decorative technique was gold tooling, which European bookbinders adopted in the fifteenth century. Muslim craftsmen, however, had used the technique as early as 1339. Gold tooling (also known as gilt tooling) involves the hand-application of extremely thin flakes of gold to the leather cover of a book. The flakes are pressed into place, resulting in delicate and beautiful designs. Bolder metallic decoration was also used, as, for example, the brass coverings on the four corners of a book, which protected it from wear.

Block Books: No Type Required

Medieval manuscript books were the product of prodigious individual labor. This effort would be greatly reduced with the introduction of moveable type and the printing press, but before Gutenberg came onto the scene with these innovations, a technique known as block printing was used. Block books can be thought of as an intermediate form between manuscript and printed books. They were made by cutting a design onto a wooden block—or more specifically, cutting away the wood that was not part of the design, leaving the image or text raised (and in reverse). The raised design was then inked and impressed on parchment or paper. Most block books contained just images, no text, and these were often crude and unsophisticated. The point of the book was not to present an artistic masterpiece, but to relate a story through pictures.

Block books—also known as xylographic books—were known in Japan and China prior to the eighth century, but the earliest extant example from Europe dates from 1423 (though scholars believe they were being made even earlier in Germany and Holland). Among the most famous of these books was the *Biblia Pauperum*, or *Bible of the Poor*, a book with numerous images depicting biblical events in the Old and New Testament. It was, simply put, an illustrated Bible. Friars used the work when ministering to those who were not literate, with the images—rather than text—conveying the message to parishioners. Some block books, however, did have text alongside images, though the words and images did not always correspond.

Though a significant amount of time went into creating each wooden block, their life span was fairly limited. With each impression the quality of the image declined. As the raised wooden images blurred, what text there was became increasingly illegible. Selecting a very hard wood to carve the image preserved the integrity of the image for a time, but the sheer pressure of the press ultimately limited the longevity of these woodblocks, thus making block books a less than ideal way to mass-produce information.

Illuminations and Illustrations

Block books were an important way to bring together images and text, but they were only part of the artistic tradition of book illustration. Today we are used to seeing pictures of extremely high quality, the result of sophisticated photographic and computer technologies, in books. However, before the age of print—when the work was done by hand and parchment was scarce—illustrations were quite uncommon. In fact, books in western Europe not only lacked pictures, but sentences were not separated from one another with spaces or punctuation; there was one solid page of text after another. For a reader this posed a real challenge: it took significant effort to discern where one sentence ended and another began. The solution scribes arrived at, at least initially, was to make the first letter of each sentence either a different size or a different color, most often red. The process of coloring capital letters red was called rubricating, from the Latin word *rubrica* for red earth. From this simple beginning, the use of increasingly decorated capital letters became fashionable in medieval manuscripts.

Once the scribe had finished copying a text he would hand it over to an artist, or illuminator, who would color and decorate the capital letters. They could mix colors, experiment with dyes and brushes, and carefully apply their craft to the manuscripts that scribes brought them. In medieval Europe, exotic blues were obtained from lapis lazuli stones, then known to exist only in central Asia. European illuminators obtained these stones through trade with their Muslim neighbors.

Ornamented capital letters were simultaneously aesthetic and a means of highlighting parts of the text. As illustrations became more common and were incorporated into the text, the reader's experience was augmented by visual cues. The earliest European texts illustrated with woodcuts appeared in the fourteenth century, though, again, the technique had been around in China almost as long as paper.

Woodcuts are, fundamentally, a simple idea. However, the process of cutting away the wood so that what remains standing is the desired image requires great skill. Moreover, the carving must be a mirror image of the anticipated illustration, since it reverses when transferred to parchment. Crude woodcuts were not hard to produce, but to achieve even a slightly artistic representation of depth and shading required a skilled craftsman. Because the image created on parchment was a black line on a white background, woodcutting is also known as the "black line method."

When the woodcut was ready for printing, it was set aside until the text was prepared. The scribe, having finished his copying, left an open space where the woodcut impression was to be made. If it was to be colored, this was added by hand later. The oldest known European woodcut dates from 1418 and, not surprisingly, depicts a religious theme. By the mid-fifteenth century, woodcuts were being used to illustrate entire books. This artistic achievement peaked with the masters of the sixteenth century, when artists such as Albrecht Dürer set new standards for woodcutting. His sixteen woodcuts of the *Apocalypse*—discussed in greater detail later—are among the best known of the late fifteenth century.

Script: Letters with Style

In the modern age of word processors, we have hundreds of fonts at our fingertips. The size of the font (such as 12 point), the style (roman, italic, bold), and the type itself (Garamond, Times New Roman, Arial) are easily modified with a simple mouse-click. Amid such a wealth of technology, it is easy to take for granted the challenges scribes faced when producing written material for a book. Before moveable type was used, books were collections of handwritten pages; thus the name manuscript, from the Latin *manus* for hand, and *script* for writing. Those trained for careers in copying were known as scribes, and their task was writing out each word with a perfectly consistent hand over the course of hundreds of pages, if not volumes. Inside their hallowed *scriptoria*, a room within the monastery where only scribes could go, texts were copied under the watchful eye of the *Armarius*—the medieval librarian.

Today, handwriting varies widely from person to person, and in many schools the craft of penmanship has gone by the wayside, replaced with typing or simply taken for granted in a computer age. But ancient and medieval scribes had a much more demanding task: each letter they wrote had to be drawn in a specific way, and if several scribes shared the task of copying a book, there should be no discernible difference in their scripts. Such accuracy was made possible through careful training in a few alphabetic models that were widely shared and were familiar to most readers.

The details of script development could fill volumes, and the study of handwriting has spawned its own field of history. But no account can ignore the influential first representation of letters, which came from Roman buildings erected throughout the empire. The letters Romans carved reflected their architectural aesthetic style, boldly standing out with limited curvature and easily legible. Roman letters are neat, with clean lines that appeal to the eye. Variations on the Roman capitals developed, some in lowercase and others with a slant, but the Roman capital letters, called majuscules, were the most widely known.

In the fourth century, about the same time parchment was replacing papyrus as the preferred writing surface, a variation in letters emerged. The smoother surface of the parchment, coupled with the use of a quill as a writing implement, meant that letters could be drawn closer together, and with greater clarity. A new script emerged, called "uncials." Found in numerous Greek and Latin manuscripts, uncials were more rounded than the Roman majuscules, with letters written one *uncia*—or Roman inch—apart. From the fourth century through the eighth, uncial script was preferred by scribes, in part because the curved shape of the letters allowed them to be written quickly, with fewer pen strokes, than the more squared Roman letters.

The next great turn in the formation of letters came in the late eighth century, when Charlemagne ordered an English scholar to develop a new script. It is difficult to imagine producing a consistent set of letters that would replace the script used for hundreds of years, but such was Charlemagne's ambition. The result was named after his Latinized name: Carolingian script, or Caroline minuscule. This script offered clear, easily read letters, similar in ways to an older form of Roman cursive but also influenced by a script known as half-uncial (a combination of uncial and cursive scripts used in Ireland around the seventh century). The Carolingian script was soon adopted by scribes across Europe—save for those in Ireland, who maintained their own style—and it provides the basis both for modern handwriting and for the commonly used Roman type. Indeed, it was Renaissance scholars who—mistakenly thinking Caroline minuscule was from antiquity—labeled it Roman script.

Because of its clarity, Caroline minuscule remained in use for centuries until scribes of the twelfth century introduced a new, more rigid letter formation known as Gothic script. Developed to save space on the paper by putting letters closer together, this script (called "Black Letter" in England and "Textur" in Germany) was angular and sharp, the letters appearing as if their stems had been broken off at the bottom and top. There were no smooth, rounded edges, thus giving the letters a bold appearance, reflective of medieval architecture. Manuscripts written in the Gothic script look very different than their minuscule predecessors. Gothic letters were the most commonly used form of writing in Europe until the Renaissance, and continued to be the preferred style in parts of northern Europe, such as Germany, until the eighteenth century.

It was the clear hand of Renaissance scholars, however, that redefined the way books appeared on the eve of the age of print. When the printing press did arrive, the pieces of type produced were carved in such a way as to mimic the hand of Renaissance humanists. Type, in its earliest manifestation, was considered successful only if you could not tell it apart from script. Today, any teacher who receives a paper printed in a font that resembles handwriting will almost assuredly turn it back and request something that looks "typed," but such an aesthetic was a long time coming.

HOMES AND READERS

From antiquity to the present, books have been collected in various places, both public and private. While storage may seem like a mundane aspect of a book's life, the fact remains that where books were housed reveals a great deal about their role in society, their accessibility to readers, and their value to owners. Between 1200 and 1400, books found their way from the vestibule of monasteries to the private libraries of wealthy Italian merchants, where they were placed next to paintings and other works of art. This journey, and the cultural influences that allowed it to take place, shed light on the book's many roles in Western society.

The places where books were housed is a good indication of readership. The history of reading is an area that has grown tremendously in the last decade, and it would be impossible here to do more than briefly summarize a few major points. But understanding the composition and demands of the readership is vital to understanding how the technologies of the books evolved.

Good demographic studies exist that can tell us how many readers there were in ancient Egypt, how many books were held in the Alexandrian library, how many booksellers there were in ancient Rome, and so forth. For our purposes it is enough to know that up to the development of the printing press, the audience for books was remarkably small. In the days of ancient Rome, noblemen and wealthy patrons collected books and exchanged them through book merchants. This of course is the story of western Europe. In Asia and the Middle East, the book trade was already flourishing, and the art and technology that went into the creation of books was quite advanced. As we have already seen, it was not until the Muslim and Christian worlds encountered each other that the West was able to appropriate many of the technologies long in use in China, Japan, and northern Africa.

Libraries

With vast collections of manuscripts and printed books, libraries have become symbols of a culture's values, practical resources for scholars, and community spaces where the public can seek out information. Like many of our great cultural institutions, the concept of the library can be traced back to the ancient Greeks. The Greek world was a scholarly hub and books were central to its culture. Under Alexander the Great, and his successors—the two Ptolemies—the library that was built at Alexandria grew to house an enormous collection of Greek literature. Estimated to hold approximately 700,000 scrolls, it included seminal works in astronomy, mathematics, philosophy, and medicine. The collection was a public recognition of the importance of writing and literacy, and scrolls collected there represented the sum total of learning in the Greek world. Scholars and authors from all over the Mediterranean region sought out the library for work, creating in Alexandria a great intellectual center.

The library's presence in Alexandria had the additional effect of stimulating trade in scrolls, since copies of works in its collection were made available for individuals to purchase. Thus, some of these papyrus manuscripts found themselves in private libraries, the smaller collections of teachers and scholars. Unfortunately, much of the Alexandrian collection was burned when Caesar conquered the region in 47 C.E. Though scrolls were acquired by the library after that fire, it suffered continued attack from Roman Emperors, and was finally destroyed in 640 C.E. by Arab invaders.

A second great ancient library was built in Asia Minor, in the western kingdom of Pergamum. King Attalus I (269–197 B.C.E.) ordered the library to be built, and it was later expanded upon by Eumenes II (197–159 B.C.E.), the same king who had called for an alternative to papyrus. Though not as large as that of Alexandria, the Pergamum library still housed a valuable collection of some 200,000 works, many of which were written on vellum. It is said that when Marc Antony fell in love with the Egyptian queen Cleopatra, he offered her all 200,000 volumes in the Pergamum library as a sign of his affection.

Other libraries existed throughout the ancient world. In Rome, both public and private libraries were to be found. A good collection of scrolls was a sign of wealth and prestige. The Roman philosopher Seneca (d. 65 C.E.) was actually critical of those who collected books just to own them, without ever applying themselves to the contents. Such a view, however, could not overcome the pleasure people found in owning, browsing, and displaying scrolls. Often, they were housed in a special room in the aristocratic Roman home.

With the rise of Christendom in the second century C.E., the church became the primary source of book production, and remained so throughout the Middle Ages. In the mid-fifteenth century Pope Nicholas V oversaw construction of a new public library in Rome, which we know now as the Vatican library. Readily accessible to clerics, scholars, and laymen in the city, the library held (and still holds) one of the greatest collections of manuscripts in the world. A hint to its perceived value was its rapid growth: in 1443, before Nicholas's tenure, a smaller papal library held 340 manuscripts (two in Greek). By 1455, upon Nicholas's death, the collection had more than tripled to 1,500 codices. By 1475 there were 2,527 manuscripts, increasing to 3,500 in 1481.

Following in this tradition, monasteries throughout Europe became repositories for thousands of books. The Benedictines were especially noted for their vast collections. Records indicate that a monastery in Durham, England, housed approximately 336 volumes, while two hundred years later, two monasteries at Canterbury listed over 3,000 titles in their collection. Public access to these collections was limited, but literate scholars were often privileged to use monastic texts. Theft was prevented by chaining books to the desks.

Mosques

Libraries, both religious and secular, were a key site for the collection of books in the West. In the East, however, books were generally housed in religious facilities. By the middle of the eighth century, the Umayyad Empire had developed a rich, literate culture in which books played a central role. These books were housed in several places: mosques, madrasas (religious schools), and private residences. Mosques were the central religious sites of Islam, yet they offered both religious and secular learning opportunities. Students—both male and female—who attended a mosque could read the Koran, as well as books on science, philosophy and poetry, and rhetoric. Indeed, non-Muslims were welcome in mosques for all areas of study except the Koran and the *hadith*, or sayings of the Prophet. There were at least 3,000 mosques in Baghdad in the tenth century, a testimony to their central role in medieval Muslim life.

Slightly different in focus were the madrasas (meaning "places for learning"). These were advanced schools that first came to be widely attended in the eleventh century. Ultimately, the madrasas transformed into universities with their own libraries. Together with local libraries, tutoring houses, palace schools, and private libraries, madrasas offered the Muslim public significant access to books. This stands in stark contrast to the western tradition, where most books were housed in monasteries, and most readers were from the clergy.

Universities

Medieval monasteries housed the majority of Europe's books until the twelfth century. The root of the word monastery is *monos*, meaning "alone." It is no surprise, then, that the majority of Europe's books were inaccessible to all but a few monks and members of the clergy who read them for the liturgical—or in some cases grammatical—information they contained. Until 1000 C.E., most learned men in Europe were associated with a monastery, their education shaped by religious dogma and clerical activities. But the twelfth century saw the founding of the first universities, and they quickly became a second important site of book acquisition and accumulation. More secular than monasteries, these institutions offered courses in the seven liberal arts (grammar, rhetoric, dialectic, arithmetic, geometry, astronomy, and music). Students who completed coursework earned degrees very similar to today's Bachelor and Master of Arts, although initially, their instruction took place at various cathedrals, instead of in established buildings. Both masters and students identified themselves as part of an educational craft—or guild—and therefore adopted the common term for a guild, *universitatis*, meaning "whole" or "totality." Over time, the guild concept was dropped, classrooms were erected, and the term university was used to identify the institution of higher learning.

As the university system grew, a new audience for books emerged: hundreds of students, who were neither monks nor churchmen (though they could become so after graduation), sought books for their intellectual edification. Unlike today's undergraduates, who can easily go to the bookstores and purchase their texts or take advantage of computers to download information for their classes, medieval students had extremely limited access to written materials. Their books could never be purchased. Instead, their texts were kept in the classrooms, often chained to desks (as in monasteries), and almost always shared by classmates. They were, after all, the product of hundreds of hours of labor. These early secular texts were often written on paper because it was cheaper and these books were not valued as much as liturgical works.

Moreover, the books were extremely large. Folio volumes (where the original sheets of paper were full-size and not folded) could easily be 2 feet tall, weigh 10 pounds, and reflect thousands of man-hours of copying and illustrating. Even if it were allowed, these books were too cumbersome for a student to take back to his room. In a traditional medieval classroom, the professor would read from the book to students. His reading—in Latin, *lectura*—was recorded by his students.

The collections of books built by universities such as Oxford, Cambridge, and Bologna were impressive. At the University of Paris, where Aristotle's works were emphasized, over a dozen Aristotelian works were being assigned in the curriculum and were therefore housed at the university (Daly 1961, 83). These universities provided a significant home for books, a tradition that continues in today's institutions.

Private Studies

Clerics and early university students were not the only people reading books in the period before the printing press. There was also an audience of wealthy patrons and aristocratic collectors who placed great value on books and sought out rare or important copies for their personal libraries. Medical and legal books, along with books of poetry and scripture, were among the most popular. In the tenth century, the Countess of Anjou in France reportedly paid 200 sheep, three barrels of grain, and several furs just for a book of sermons. Clearly, at this juncture, books were not readily available to the general public. It was not until paper began to replace parchment in the fourteenth century that books became more affordable and started to circulate among a wider audience.

Learned aristocrats built libraries, or studies, where their collections of unique and rare works served as a testimony to both their wealth and intellect. Cardinal Bessarion (1389–1472), an important member of the church and a renowned scholar, had a private collection of at least 800 volumes, many of which were translated from Greek by him. The king of Hungary, Matthias Corvinus (r. 1458–1490) had a collection of over 500 volumes, and the Italian humanist Giovanni Pico della Mirandola (1463–1494) had at least 1,000 volumes in his library at the time he died (King 2005, 67). In an age in which each volume represented months of scribes' labor, these early collections testify to the importance of books as cultural objects.

THE EVE OF THE RENAISSANCE

In the biography of the book, medieval monasteries deserve credit for creating large libraries, for preserving rare works, and for taking the book from its ancient form into an elaborate and highly ornamented art. But by the fourteenth century medieval bookmaking—indeed, the very basis for the book's existence—was changing. A new era—the Renaissance—marked a decisive change in the way books were made, circulated, and read.

With its roots in fourteenth-century Italy, the cultural and intellectual rebirth known as the Renaissance pulled Europe away from many medieval traditions. In a complex way, the Renaissance affected people's values, their view of the world, and the kinds of knowledge they sought. At the center of this change was an ideology known as humanism: the notion that man should seek out and embrace new knowledge, and that this knowledge could and should be excavated from the classical past—from ancient Greece and Rome. Renaissance humanists rejected the entrenched methods of the medieval period, and moved away from the moribund scholarly techniques of monks, who focused almost exclusively on religious works. Rather, as one scholar of the period writes, humanists

> wrote letters, speeches, treatises, dialogues, plays, poems, and histories; they were philosophers, theologians, bureaucrats, and mathematicians. . . . Between 1350 and 1530, the Italian humanists put into circulation a wealth of ideas that linked their present with the classical past and opened up the main lines of intellectual inquiry for centuries to come. (King 2005, 66)

The stacks of books in monastic libraries reflected, to Renaissance humanists, just so many dead ends in man's pursuit of wisdom, a sentiment that inspired them to both write their own books as well as gather books from classical antiquity. The leading ideology of the Renaissance, then, was humanism, and its icon was the book.

Beginning in the latter half of the fourteenth century, books would be transformed both inside and out. Physically they would move away from the large tomes chained to monastic desks, becoming smaller, more portable, volumes. But more importantly, their content would become increasingly secular as the audience for them evolved. Books of the medieval period covered an array of topics, from medicine to folklore to music, but the majority centered on the Christian Church; they were fundamentally liturgical in nature.

Renaissance scholars, freed from the shackles of ecclesiastical topics, turned instead to the writers of ancient Greece and Rome—considered by the church to be pagans, and their works, therefore, entirely incongruent with scripture. Classical works, according to the church, should be banned, and interest in them stamped out. Unfortunately for the church, Renaissance scholars found in these books a spectrum of new and fruitful topics: from nature to science, philosophy to literature, all of which they hoped to make available to a larger reading public. By the early fifteenth century, such secular books had become a portal to a new age of learning that would sweep the Western world.

Throughout Italy, wealthy patrons and aristocrats became avid collectors of ancient books and manuscripts, giving rise to a flourishing book industry. Scribes were in great demand, as patrons commissioned particular works for their libraries, often paying exorbitant rates to get books of great artistry. Monasteries and universities also needed texts and employed scribes, but the most elaborate books were—by the fifteenth century—finding their way onto aristocratic shelves.

The Medici family, famous patrons of the arts and sciences, established a major collection of books in their Florentine library. Here, scrolls from ancient Greece and codices from the days of Cicero in Rome were collected. Francesco Petrarch (1304–1374), a quintessential Renaissance figure, collected books from antiquity with a passion few matched but many copied. He was also one of the most vocal critics of the medieval appearance of books. Finding their Gothic script too awkward to read he called for something more legible. Petrarch's library held at least 200 volumes, and was among the largest in Europe at the time.

The attitudes of Renaissance intellectuals created a demand for access to information and a society ready for an improved means of transmitting that information. In short, by the mid-fifteenth century, Europe was ripe for the innovation that would make books more widely available. And in Germany, a group of men centered around the city of Mainz were preparing to take advantage of such changing intellectual tides.

2

Infancy: The Earliest Printed Books, 1450–1500

GUTENBERG: THE REPUTED GRANDFATHER

Conventional wisdom has it that Johannes Gutenberg invented printing, developed the first printing press, and even created the very first modern book. However, like much of any history that focuses on the efforts of a single individual, these credits tend to obscure actual events and fail to capture Gutenberg's very real accomplishments. In fact, as the previous chapter has shown, he invented neither books nor the idea of printing, which had been done with block books for centuries. Rather, he was one of a small group of craftsmen who developed a method of creating durable metal type quickly and consistently. It was the production of type, coupled with related innovations, that made the printing press a useful technology. For the first time, multiple impressions of a text could be made economically and with clarity, paving the way for the first information revolution.

Problematically for historians, Gutenberg left little record of his specific activities. Debate about his role in the development of printing technology continues to rage. But recent investigation of Gutenberg's efforts has amplified the work of earlier historians by adding the tools of science to traditional scholarship, uncovering fascinating new details about the origins of the printed book. This new information proves that Gutenberg's work is central to the history of books. In the life story of books, he is an important character.

Gutenberg's Contributions

Johannes Gutenberg was born in 1399 in Mainz. Known especially for its metalworkers, Mainz was a thriving city on the Rhine River in present-day Germany. Johannes's was a patrician family: while not aristocrats, they were more than common craftsmen. His father owned property—the mark of social standing—and held a key position at the local mint. From an early age, Gutenberg was exposed to metalworking and goldsmithing. In particular, his understanding of how coins were cast—how the raised impression on the coin was created—would prove critical to his later work on creating metal type.

In 1428, political conflicts between the artisan's guilds and the higher class patricians sparked Gutenberg's departure for Strasbourg, a city that still sits in medieval splendor at the junction of the Rhine and Ill Rivers. There, he began to experiment with new printing methods, sometimes referred to in documents of the period as "artificial script." Though details are not clear, it seems evident that he was working on a method of producing moveable type. He was not alone in his endeavors. Other craftsmen in Europe were also trying to devise an artificial script. It was a technology whose formative moment seemed to have arrived.

Though Gutenberg's family owned property, he was not independently wealthy and therefore had to make a living, which he did as a craftsman. Business accounts help us to understand some of the details of Gutenberg's business in Strasbourg. Though the exact nature of his work is not clear (some suggest the wine trade, others lens crafting and the making of mirrors), he is known to have taken out loans, and to have had assistants working in his shop. Whatever his primary occupation, it is evident that Gutenberg's spare time was devoted to development of printing technology. In connection with this pursuit, he also entered into a legal partnership with three other men from Strasbourg (Hans Riffe, Andres Heilmann, and Andres Dritzehen), agreeing to teach them an unspecified process, which they were bound by oath not to reveal. In return for his instruction, Gutenberg was paid a fee by these men.

Ultimately, discord within the group landed them in court in 1439—but even court papers do not reveal the secret process on which they were collaborating. Upon the death of one partner, Gutenberg issued letters requesting that certain items be melted down, and another device dismantled. On the verge of what he must have known would be a significant technological breakthrough, Gutenberg was extraordinarily cautious about protecting its design. His vision of a printing press, however, like many breakthrough technologies, would be gestating for a while.

On political and religious fronts, the fifteenth century was quite turbulent, and sometime around 1444—with Strasbourg in the grips of war—Gutenberg moved again. His whereabouts for the next four years are not well documented, but in 1448 he reappeared in Mainz to continue the printing work he had begun earlier in Strasbourg. His device must have taken on a more definite form, because between 1450 and 1453, Gutenberg took out two more loans of 800 guilders each—in modern currency, about $150,000—from a goldsmith-turned-businessman named Johann Fust. The interest on the loan was 6 percent, and Fust expressed a desire to be in a partnership with Gutenberg when the printing press was complete. Clearly, whatever technology he had developed at this point was sufficient to impress potential lenders; part of the contract even stipulated that should Gutenberg default on the loan, ownership of all the printing equipment would be transferred to Fust.

At long last, Gutenberg's ideas were brought to life in a shop run by Peter Schöffer, an engraver and calligrapher (as well as a relative of Fust) whom Gutenberg had hired to assist him. Schöffer oversaw six of Gutenberg's presses and the employees running them—two to three men per press—from 1450 to 1456. Compared to the fifty or more scribes per shop who were employed in the days of manuscript, this was a significant reduction of staff. But the new technology of moveable type increased potential production dramatically. Even in print's nascent stages, Gutenberg was working on several projects simultaneously. Among these were a popular Latin grammar book known as the *Donatus* and a printed calendar for the year 1455. Though none of the extant copies bear his name, several are attributable to him based on detailed physical analysis of the type.

End of a Partnership

Gutenberg had proved that the press was not just functional but revolutionary. But on the verge of success, Gutenberg and Fust became embroiled in a lawsuit. The details may never be fully understood, but apparently, the printing project was developing too slowly for Fust, who foreclosed on Gutenberg in 1455, demanding repayment of his loans plus the interest. Fust may have been concerned about long-term profitability, or perhaps he simply wanted to wrest control of the printing equipment from Gutenberg, who, some scholars suggest, was diverting money from the Schöffer concern into a different project. What exactly transpired is unclear, but legal papers record the outcome.

The courts ruled in Fust's favor. Gutenberg was found to have defaulted on the loan. He was in no position to remedy the situation, and in 1457 he was forced to surrender most of the printing equipment he had been working on for years. At the very moment Gutenberg realized his vision, he lost everything, including most of his type and copies of works he had printed thus far (Man 2002, 189–190). His shop foreman, Peter Schöffer, inherited the presses and—in a newly-formed partnership with Fust—set up the equipment in a shop of his own.

Was Gutenberg the victim of a conspiracy between Schöffer and Fust? Fust had adopted Schöffer as a youth and sent him to Paris for training as a calligrapher and engraver. Installation of his surrogate in Gutenberg's shop would have guaranteed him inside knowledge of the most intimate details of the printing process—Gutenberg's "intellectual property." Fust's relationship with Schöffer was cemented by the latter's marriage to Fust's daughter. Schöffer inherited the presses and Gutenberg was left with just a small amount of type.

Fust's lawsuit against Gutenberg, while unfortunate for Gutenberg, did not hinder the development of printed books. On the contrary, Fust and Schöffer combined their technical expertise and business acumen to produce some of the earliest and most elegantly printed books of Mainz, on the very presses Gutenberg had labored so long to develop.

Gutenberg's Bible

So what of Gutenberg's efforts? Though his contribution to the technology of print was tremendous, there are no books extant today that bear his name. Court and financial records allow the presumption that he was using his funds to print books with his new presses. But only through historical forensics can we actually prove that Gutenberg was really responsible for the accomplishments that are attributed to him. Sophisticated microscopy allows the tracing of the type found in various books back to the workshop that originated them. Thus, experts in typography have concluded that the type found in the famous Gutenberg Bible indeed belonged to the man for whom it was named. Modern technology is helping to clarify Gutenberg's place in the early development of the printed book.

Gutenberg's Bible, as were many of the earliest printed books, was in Latin. It was an appropriate work for the first major printing project. It embodied all the innovations of a new technology, while at the same time retaining the artistry and craftsmanship reminiscent of the manuscript era.

Would retention of traditional manuscript forms make this volume more marketable? Possibly—and marketability had certainly been on Gutenberg's mind.

A copy of this Bible held in the Bibliothèque Nationale in Paris contains a handwritten note in the back—written by the rubricator and binder—which indicates that it was finished in Mainz on August 24, 1456. The Bible consists of 641 leaves (or 1282 pages) and is divided into two volumes. Each page measures 16.5 × 12 inches. The text is organized into two columns per page, each column with forty-two lines—and thus it is often referred to as the forty-two-line Bible. Copies exist, however, that have only forty lines per page. Historians have concluded that Gutenberg started with slightly larger pieces of type, but then shaved down the tops and bottoms of the individual pieces. By reducing the amount of white space between each line of text, he found he could save significant amounts of paper. Adding the extra two lines per page saved thirty leaves of paper per copy, a 5 percent savings overall. This minor alteration is evidence of how rapidly the technology would evolve.

The type Gutenberg used in the Bible is called *textura*: Gothic-looking letters intended to mimic the handwriting of scribes. Indeed, this Bible is hardly recognizable as a printed work without close examination of each letter. While the individual letters were consistent throughout the book, the capital letters that began each sentence and chapter were individually colored—or rubricated—by hand. The marginal decorations, with their brilliant allegorical images, were also done by hand. Thus, the uniformity introduced by the press did not preclude the uniqueness of each individual Bible.

It is estimated that the original print run of Gutenberg's Bible was 180 copies. Of these, 140 were on paper and 40 on vellum. This meant Gutenberg purchased about 5,000 calfskins for the vellum copies and at least 50,000 sheets of paper—a significant investment that he could only hope to recoup through later sales (Thorpe 1999, 29). At least forty-eight copies are extant today (thirty-six on paper, twelve on vellum), and scholars continue to study their slight variations for clues about their production.

After printing the Bible, Gutenberg is thought to have worked on a second major project—printed initially in 1460—called the *Mainz Catholicon*. A popular and lengthy Latin encyclopedia, the *Catholicon* was originally written in the thirteenth century by Johann Balbus, and was much sought after by clerics who valued it as an instructional manual. The pages of this book were the same size as those in the forty-two-line Bible, but the type was different—rounder than the Bible's Gothic type and about one-third smaller. Scholars debate the details of the *Catholicon*'s production but it is

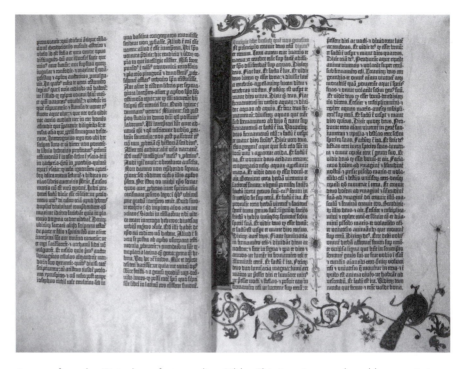

A page from the Gutenberg forty-two-line Bible. This item is reproduced by permission of The Huntington Library, San Marino, California.

certain that several editions were printed, including some after Gutenberg's death, indicating that the type was probably purchased by at least one printer after the original print run.

There is, however, a colophon—or printer's note—at the end of the *Catholicon*, which proudly attributes the work to a Mainz print shop, but offers no clue as to its printer:

> With the help of the Most High at whose will the tongues of infants become eloquent . . . this noble book *Catholicon* has been printed and accomplished without the help of reed, stylus, or pen but by the wondrous agreement, proportion and harmony of punches and types, in the year of the Lord's incarnation 1460 in the noble city of Mainz of the renowned German nation . . .

This was not the first recorded colophon. But, if Gutenberg's, it testifies to the printer's awareness of his accomplishment. He understood the impact of the new technology and took pride in it. Perhaps the colophon can be read as a direct response to those who sought to take credit for Gutenberg's invention.

Aside from the colophon, Gutenberg's book lacked many of the things we expect to see in a book today: a title page, a table of contents, an index, a reference to the printing house, copyright, or pagination. To the modern reader, these are a book's identifiers—a guide to a book's origins and to its contents. But to a fifteenth-century scribe or printer, such paratext was waste of paper—a precious commodity. Therefore, in the early days of printing, with readers relatively few in number, such details were unknown.

Little is known about Gutenberg after 1460. He died in Mainz on February 3, 1468. Shortly after his death, a Sorbonne professor named Guillaume Fichet penned a brief tribute to this integral figure in the history of printing. His comments appeared in a letter printed in December 1470, characterizing Gutenberg as the person who,

> first of all men, devised the art of printing, whereby books are made, not by a reed, as did the ancients, nor with a quill pen, as do we, but with metal letters, and that swiftly, neatly, beautifully. Surely this man is worthy to be loaded with divine honors by all the Muses, all the arts, all the tongues of those who delight in books, and is all the more to be preferred to gods and goddesses in that he has put the means of choice within reach of letters themselves and of mortals devoted to culture. (Thorpe 1999, 31)

Fust and Schöffer

The first book off the press of Fust and Schöffer—the inheritors of Gutenberg's shop—is known as the *Mainz Psalter*, a famous 1457 printing of the Psalms as they were traditionally sung in church. Historians remain unclear as to how much of this work should be attributed to Gutenberg, but by the time it was sold, Fust was the printer in charge.

The *Psalter* is extraordinary in several ways. It is the first example of color printing, with blue and red ink used on the initial capital letters, and red ink alone used on the first letter of each sentence. The latter effort is another reminder of how closely early printers sought to mimic the efforts of scribes and rubricators of the manuscript era. Multicolored printing was accomplished by pressing the same sheet multiple times. The press was lowered onto a character partially inked with blue, and then again onto the same character partially inked with red—all after the black text had already been printed. A second innovation of the *Psalter* is the appearance of two new typefaces among its 350 pages; again, evidence of how rapidly the appearance of the printed book was evolving, even in its earliest days.

Finally, the *Psalter* contained the first example of the printer's note, or colophon, mentioned earlier in relation to the *Catholicon*. The colophon of the manuscript era referred to the last words written in a book. In the first printed books it identified the printer, as well as the date and place of publication. While modern books offer this information on the title page (typically at the bottom, after the title and author), the first colophons were located at the back of the book. Gutenberg would have been disappointed to read Fust and Schöffer's colophon:

> The present copy of the Psalms, adorned with venerable capital letters and also distinguished by appropriate rubrications, was so fashioned thanks to the ingenious discovery of imprinting and forming letters without any use of a pen and completed with diligence to the glory of God by Johann Fust, citizen of Mainz, and Peter Schöffer of Gernsheim, in the year of our Lord 1457 . . .

Five years later, Fust and Schöffer printed an edition of Gutenberg's Latin Bible. This Bible was the first book to have a printer's device, a logo representing the book's house of origin. Other printers adopted this custom, and printer's devices quickly became associated with specific presses.

COMPONENTS OF INNOVATION: TYPE, PRESSES, INK, AND PAPER

From the earliest stages, the technology of the printing press was being utilized and improved upon by several individuals, often simultaneously and in different places. Though Gutenberg has received much credit for the key developments, the truth is that a host of craftsmen, with different skills and specialties, were collectively turning the idea of printed books into a reality. The network of artisans and innovators who made printing viable was an expansion of the web of technologies that were involved. In what follows, we will examine the elements that culminated in the printed book.

Making Moveable Type

Impressions were made on paper long before the fifteenth century. Block books, mentioned earlier, are a good example of this, though frequently, what was being printed from the blocks of wood was a series of images that were used in playing cards, calendars, and informational flyers. So, the idea of duplicating an impression by pulling the handle of a press did not arrive de novo with Gutenberg and his fellow Mainz craftsmen.

But what about creating individual pieces of type? Again, this had been invented long before, by the Chinese, who in the eleventh century created type from baked clay. Their efforts, however, never became part of the Asian print tradition because language posed a pragmatic challenge. The Chinese language consists of over 5,000 characters, or ideograms, which could be arranged in thousands of ways. Creating that many individual pieces of type was simply not practical, and efforts to develop moveable type were abandoned. But the European alphabet, with only twenty-six characters, was far better suited to the invention. The challenge was to find a way to efficiently create individual pieces of type, which could then be assembled and used in a press.

Initial efforts in this direction involved carving letters in relief on either wood or metal, and using these letters as stamps to make alphabetic impressions on parchment. Lined up in a frame, such carved letters could be arranged to print an entire page. This process, however, presented significant problems. Each new letter carved by hand varied slightly from its mates, meaning that the printed work would lack uniformity. For example, the letter P would look a bit different in each place it appeared, since each was carved individually. Moreover, the quality of the impression would decline rapidly because the pressure of the press affected the integrity of the type, particularly those letters carved from wood. Ultimately, using a press to print rudimentary carved letters was hardly more efficient than—and certainly not qualitatively superior to—using scribes to copy a work.

Gutenberg's real contribution, then, was not the actual invention of moveable pieces of type, but a practical solution to the problem of creating moveable metal type quickly and accurately. With this accomplished, the printing press became a viable technology for the rapid production of books.

Gutenberg's experiences working with gold and other metals, as well as his familiarity with the casting of coins, gave him the kind of background needed to come up with an effective typecasting instrument—a mold into which molten metal could be poured, giving it the shape of a letter of the alphabet or a symbol used in writing. There are four steps involved in the manufacture of moveable type. First, the creation of a negative impression in hard metal, the "punch," for each character to be printed. Second, using the punch to create a positive impression in soft metal, the "matrix," which could serve as the model for the creation of multiple pieces of identical type. Third, placing the matrix in a vessel called a "mold," capable of receiving molten metal. And fourth, arranging the newly made pieces of type in a form in order to compose text on a page.

Each of these steps presented Gutenberg and his fellow craftsmen with a complex set of problems to solve. To begin, a type-cutter or typecaster must make a model of the letter he wants on the tip of a long steel punch. The task involves multiple specialized tools, such as files, gravers, and a counter-punch, which together help the type-cutter carve out the interior and exterior of a letter. For example, if the letter Q were desired, he would select a counterpunch with a rounded O-shape and strike the punch with it to make a rounded impression that is the center of the letter Q. But the punch would still only look like a rod of metal with a hole in it. To complete the letter, the type-cutter would use gravers and files of various sizes (the smaller, the more accurate) to shave down the metal on the exterior of the Q, leaving the actual lines that make up the letter raised up in relief on the punch.

If punches vary in height, width, or length, the pieces of type that are ultimately created will be uneven, and the final printed page will lack uniformity. Creating punches is the most critical step in the process of making moveable type. But goldsmiths of the period frequently used such methods in the production of stamps and coins, having learned such exacting techniques during their apprenticeships.

The punch was then used as a stamp in the second step of the process. The punch was set on top of another piece of metal—a softer alloy like brass or copper that would take an impression. The craftsman tapped the end of the punch with a hammer, driving its raised letter into the metal beneath it, creating a recessed impression of the letter on the punch. This is known as the *matrix*, from a Latin word that means mother, because from this impression all the other pieces of type will be made. Printers would later call the impression-generating punch the *patrix*. Great skill was required to ensure that each letter punched into the matrix was of the same height as the others, otherwise uneven type heights would result. To achieve uniform letter heights, the typecaster sometimes filed down the surface around the recessed letter, ensuring that when matrices were lined up, they would be on the same level.

The third step in the creation of a piece of type is possibly the most ingenious. The matrix is set between two pieces of a mold, called "forms," that fit together perfectly to make a seal. The matrix sits at the bottom of the mold, held in place with a spring. When the mold is closed there remains only a small opening at the top, ready to receive the molten metal.

The liquefied metal, a mixture of lead, tin, and antimony, is at around 600 degrees Fahrenheit. Arriving at the proper ratio of these ingredients no doubt took some time, and no little risk, given that antimony is highly toxic. Metallurgists like Gutenberg exercised great caution when heating it up in the small confines of their shops, lest they inhale too much of this substance, and a steady hand was needed to pour it into the hand-sized mold. Caution also had to be exercised in pouring the metal into the mold. Not only were burns a potential problem—especially since the metal was simply poured from a ladle—but the angle at which the metal hit the matrix affected the shape of the piece of type created. Consistency in pouring was developed through much practice.

The advantage of the lead-tin-antimony alloy is that it hardens quickly, so that within seconds of being poured into the mold, it sets and cools. Gutenberg and his fellow typecasters could open up the mold right after pouring, and find inside the hardened piece of type, approximately 4 cm long. On the end was a letter in relief, just as it appeared on the original punch. This piece of type, called a "sort," could be reproduced to create an entire set of letters that looked exactly alike, and doing so did not take much time. Men who cast type for a living could create four sorts per minute, meaning thousands of sorts could be produced each day.

The Press: From Wine and Olives to Paper

The printing presses used in Gutenberg's era were descendants of those that had been used for hundreds of years to press olives or grapes. Adapted to printmaking, they were known as "platen" presses, after the German word for the plate that applies the pressure. Cumbersome but simple, they had been used before the arrival of moveable type to make woodcut impressions. Gutenberg's press worked like a vise with a screw mechanism, applying firm and even pressure on a piece of moist paper that sat atop the inked type. It was critical that the surface of the type—each individual letter—be the same height. Otherwise, the impression on paper would be uneven: some letters dark and potentially smudged, others too light to read. But sorts deteriorated at different rates, the more frequently used letters being worn more quickly. To ensure an even impression despite slightly uneven type, printers stretched felt (or extra pieces of paper) across an iron frame called a "tympan" and then placed the blank paper to be printed on top of this felt. That way, as the platen was pulled down onto the bed of type, there was a slight "give" behind the paper, which allowed each sort to transfer its impression equally.

The arranged type (about which more will be said later) was set in a "chase"—a frame that holds the assembled pieces of type together. This chase rested on the "bed" of the press, which slid beneath the platen on horizontal tracks. Once it was in position, the pressman turned the screw, lowering the platen and applying pressure to the inked surface. Because ink had a tendency to splatter or bleed onto the white space of the page, another device called the "frisket" was used. Shaped like a window frame, the frisket was a mat that fit around the perimeter of the typed portion of the page, protecting the margins from ink. It also secured the paper to the tympan.

Once the impression was made, the pressman retracted the screw, raising the platen, and the bed was rolled out from beneath the press. The frisket and tympan were raised and the newly inked paper carefully removed and hung to dry.

The concept of the press is simple, but the operation complex. And as printers made improvements and modifications—altering the press to suit their individual needs—its complexity only increased.

The Chemistry of Ink

Printers also faced the problem of finding an ink that would evenly cover the metallic letters and produce readable and durable text on the page. Scribes had been writing almost exclusively on calf- or sheepskins. For them, a water-based ink was an adequate medium. Printers, however, were working on a different substrate—paper—and their research led them to an ink consisting of two basic components: a liquid varnish and a solid pigment. The varnish, made from a combination of linseed oil, soot, and amber, had for years been used by Flemish painters. The oily nature of this ink gave it a thickness suitable for clinging to metal type, and also prevented it from spreading too much once it was applied to the paper. Composition of the pigment was dependent on the color involved.

For black ink, the color was derived by purifying soot, so that the oils and tars were removed and a pure black powder remained. This powder was then added to the varnish, providing the pigmentation. Science, however, has revealed even more about these high-quality inks. British chemists who carefully studied the black and colored inks of the Gutenberg Bible have determined that the reflective quality of the black ink is due to its high metallic content, including copper, lead, and titanium.

While the text of Gutenberg's Bible was printed on his press, the illustrations and rubrications were done by hand. Here, too, Gutenberg had to determine the best ink for illuminators to use. Cinnabar (mercuric sulfide) was employed for making red, and the mineral lapis lazuli for creating the vivid blues. The beauty of these inks came at a price, and as the market for printing became more competitive, the quality of inks had to be sacrificed in order to reduce the cost of a print job. Books printed shortly after those of the original Mainz trio—Gutenberg, Fust, and Schöffer—lacked both the richness of color and the longevity of the original inks. By the sixteenth century, there would be specialist ink manufacturers who serviced print shops throughout Europe, typically with inks that cost one-third to one-quarter of what the ink in the Gutenberg Bible had cost (Gaskell 1995, 126).

Readying the Paper

Ink and type are only two parts of the equation that led to the technology known as the book. Paper was the third essential component. Parchment quickly fell out of favor, except in rare cases where it was sought for aesthetic reasons. As detailed in Chapter 1, paper had been brought to Europe by the Arabs, but it was not until the printing press had matured into a functional technology that demand for paper grew. More accurately, the demand increased exponentially; papermakers could scarcely keep up. Most copies of the forty-two-line Bible were printed on paper imported from a region of northern Italy known as the Piedmont, but it was not long before paper mills were well established in many major European cities, with print shops vying for the best quality at the best prices.

Paper was a significant up-front expense that often required financial backing of some kind. When ready for a new job, the printer would order the requisite amount of paper from a warehouse. It would arrive in stacks, or tokens, of 250 sheets. The night before printing began, the approximate number of sheets needed for the job were wet down and then stacked upon each other. The weight of the stack squeezed out much of the water, resulting in slightly damp sheets the next day. The moistness allowed the fibers of the paper to receive the ink in a way they would not, were they completely dry.

Taken individually from the stacks, the sheets were placed in the tympan. The frisket was then swung into place to cover the paper's margins, and then the whole unit slid beneath the platen. With a pressman's turn of the screw, the type—which had been inked with special leather pads—transferred the image to the paper. With the impression complete, the paper was removed from the press and hung to dry in the rafters of the shop.

A Gutenberg Legacy?

The history of early books—understood as pieces of technology—is today being analyzed and better comprehended through more modern technologies. For example, chemists can use spectrographic techniques to determine which of Gutenberg's Bibles were printed with the same batches of ink. Since batches were made up by hand, variations in the ink provide clues to, among other things, the order in which the books were printed.[1]

---

[1] They have also used the cyclotron to determine where—in the process of printing the Bible—new batches of ink were made. By understanding which sections of the Bible were printed together, historians gain insight into how the work was ultimately constructed. They are applying the leading technologies of the twenty-first century to better understand the leading technologies of the fifteenth.

More provocative are recent theories that the credit given to Gutenberg for the development of moveable type is undeserved (Smith 2001). A specialist in rare books, and a physicist have combined their knowledge with the power of several computers to examine the type of a document attributed to Gutenberg's press. Their analysis revealed that individual letters lacked the consistency one would expect to find in type issued from the same mold. Recall that the entire technology revolves around the ability to replicate exactly individual pieces of type. These scholars suggest that Gutenberg, instead of using a metal mold, used a sand mold, a more rudimentary technique. Sand molds are remade each time a piece of type is cast, meaning that individual letters would (upon very close examination) look slightly different.

Historians have determined that, by the 1470s, printers in Germany were using metal, not sand, molds. But whether Gutenberg should ultimately be credited with the technique remains unclear. Nonetheless, his efforts are emblematic of the work having been done in his period to introduce the book as a more advanced technology, and he will continue to be referred to here as the "Father" of the printed book.

Gutenberg and his brother printers, regardless of claims to primacy, collectively must be credited with a major synthetic achievement. They brought together innovations in ink, paper, presses, and type, which collectively had a major impact on the technology of books.

THE MIDWIVES: BRINGING A BOOK INTO THE WORLD

Producing a book required not only the hardware—presses and type—and materials—ink and paper—but also a skilled set of workers, specialists at their crafts. Images of the earliest print shops are scarce, but those that do exist provide a window through which we can understand who these craftsmen were and what they did.

Compositors

Standing at the head of the printer's "assembly line" was the compositor. The compositor's job was to first read the manuscript provided by the author and then set the type for it. It was arduous and demanding work.

The sorts were organized in cases positioned directly in front of the compositor. The upper case contained the capital letters, which were used less frequently, while the lower case contained small capitals, or what are now known simply as lowercase letters. A good compositor could memorize the location of each sort in the case, and find them without hesitation, much as a typist today knows the location of each key on a keyboard. However, each printing shop had its own unique case organization, which meant that a compositor would have to relearn the sort locations all over again every time he took on a new job. Later this would be standardized. Rendering the job more difficult, the sorts themselves became increasingly small as time went by.

As the compositor read from the manuscript, he selected letters and set them on what is called a composing stick, a trough-like metal rod into which the sorts fit snugly. Because the type had to be set in reverse (to ensure that the mirror image was printed) the composer would set the type upside down, allowing him to move it left to right. Once a line was composed on the stick, it was placed on a galley—a long tray open at one end in which a page is prepared. The side walls of the galley sit lower than the pieces of type to allow for an impression, and the rows of type are separated from each other with bars. All lines needed to be the same length in order to fit squarely in the galley, and to ensure this, additional spaces at the end of the line were filled with blank slugs—a process known as justifying the line. A filled galley is referred to as a "form," though it should not be confused with the form involved in creating pieces of type. When all the lines that could fit on a page were ready, the letters in the galley were tied together and locked into a chase so that the sorts would not slip. The chase was then placed on the bed of the press.

Not only was the compositor's work physically exacting, but depending on the work being printed, he had to have considerable language skills in Greek or Latin. In some cases, knowledge of mathematics was also necessary to avoid basic errors in setting the type. It is believed that six compositors worked for two years to set the type for Gutenberg's Bible.

Inkers

Once the form was prepared, it was transferred to the press stone: a large piece of marble that could withstand the pressure of the press without yielding. The type was inked in a process called "dyeing." This was done with two leather hemispheres, each with a handle, which were dipped in the ink and then pressed against the surface of the type. Spills and splatters were hopefully avoided, and—with the bed of type evenly inked—a damp piece of paper (typically prepared the night before) was carefully placed in the tympan, the frisket was folded over its margins, and the entire tympan/ frisket system was folded on top of the inked type.

Type was inked just before the platen was lowered to make an impression. Woodcut by Jost Amman, 1568. This item is reproduced by permission of The Huntington Library, San Marino, California.

Pressmen

Finally, a pressman pulled the bar, turning the screw that was connected to the platen and pressing the paper down onto the inked sorts. Though not the most highly skilled task in the shop, operating the press was exhausting work. The pull had to be firm enough to make the impression, but not so firm that the torque twisted the platen and smeared the ink. Images of pressmen from the earliest days of the printing press highlight their physical stature, their strong forearms, and—with their entire bodies pulling against the lever—the amount of physical effort that went into running the press.

Binders

After the pages of a book had all been printed and dried, they were folded according to the size of the book, and groups of leaves—called quires—were sewn together. (The issue of page layout and folding is dealt with in greater detail in Chapter 3.) It was not uncommon for books to be sold without bindings, though wealthy purchasers would almost always have a binding put on the book, both to protect the pages and add to its beauty as an object. The nature of bindings changed little from the period of manuscripts to that of the first printed books. Most books were bound between two wooden boards covered in tanned calf- or goatskin. These leather covers were then adorned with gold leaf, elaborate stamps, and in some cases, metal hooks or clasps were screwed into the wood to keep it shut when not being read.

Overall, binding remained a craft distinct from printing. Though in some cases a print shop would hire a binder or collaborate with a bindery in the neighborhood, it was a leather-worker's area of expertise, and printed books like those of Fust and Gutenberg were handled by someone outside the printing house.

THE FIRST-BORN: INCUNABLES

Within fifteen years of print's debut in Mainz, there was a press in every country in western Europe. Printers from German cities facilitated the spread of print by moving to other areas—Italy and France in particular—and setting up new shops. Books published in the first fifty years after Gutenberg's invention of moveable type are referred to as "incunables" (*incunabula* is Latin for cradle). Incunables are those books created in printing's infancy, when techniques of typecasting and printing were still fairly new. One characteristic of books produced in this period is their obvious level of craftsmanship, since books were still meant to look like high-quality manuscripts.

The fidelity of many of the incunables to the manuscript tradition is striking. Books from 1450 to 1480, though the product of the press, attempted to deny their own technological heritage by appearing in types that mimicked handwriting. Also, they had no title pages and were colored and illustrated by hand.

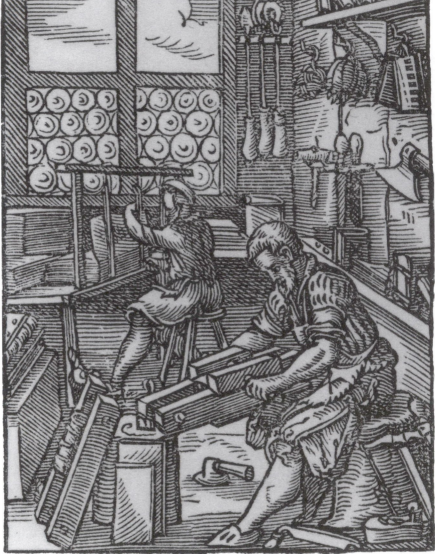

The bookbinder was responsible for sewing, pressing, and tooling each book. Woodcut by Jost Amman, 1568. This item is reproduced by permission of The Huntington Library, San Marino, California.

Imitation, however complimentary, did not appease the scribes, who constituted the most vocal critics of print technology. Their livelihood was at stake, and by all accounts their numbers had grown significantly in the

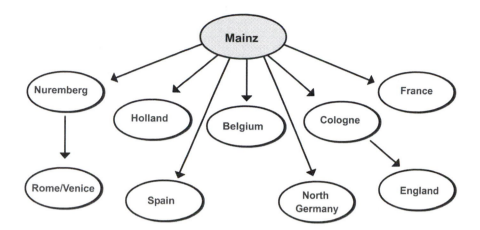

The spread of printing technology from Mainz to other European cities.

early fifteenth century in order to meet the demand for books by patrons and wealthy collectors. The printing press was a clear threat to their occupation, especially considering that books appeared to have been written by hand. Along with the scribes, guilds of engravers voiced protest over the technology of printed books, fearing that their trade would be similarly displaced by automation. In an effort to secure work, many guilds arranged for their engravers to work under contract with printers.

The Spread of Print

What is most remarkable about the history of books in this period is the speed with which the technology spread from Germany to other parts of Europe. In large part, this was due to the diaspora of printers from Mainz and other German cities. The archbishop of Mainz and his troops had sacked Mainz in 1462, contributing to an unfavorable—and unstable—business climate. The printers who left Mainz were searching both for business opportunities and for a more politically temperate environment. Moving to France or Italy allowed them to start over in cities with significant commercial potential, such as Venice, Rome, Lyon, and Paris.

Cologne was the first destination for printers leaving Mainz. They set up shop in 1464 and catered to the demands of a large student population. Such university towns provided a ready-made market for textbooks. Basel was the next city (1466), followed by Rome (1467) and Venice (1469). Paris, Nuremburg, and Utrecht had presses by 1470, and Milan, Naples, and Florence by 1471. And with each new establishment came improvements in printing technique, and an increase in the audience for printed books. Between 1450 and 1470, printing shops were opened in fourteen cities. By 1480 the number of shops had increased to over one hundred (forty-seven in Italy alone).

What had started as a craft quickly evolved into a more complicated business, with specialist typecasters, printers, paper suppliers and booksellers. Typecasters, for example, would travel to various printing shops with their molds and offer their services. Thus, the sorts created for different printing houses were often identical, since the molds and matrices used to make them were the same.

But specialization did not imply homogenization. Until the sixteenth century, books presented a variety of faces to the world. The incunables became increasingly ornamented. Printers were aware that the buyers of these books sought an object with aesthetic appeal, and they added beautiful woodcuts, ornate borders around the pages, attractive fonts, and finely crafted bindings to their products.

German Printers

Anton Koberger (1445–1513) of Nuremberg established a print shop in 1470 that would become one of the largest of the incunable period. His operation was international, connected to offices throughout Europe, and tied into business networks. While printing may have begun as a small craft business, Koberger viewed it as something more: a way to raise his social status and enter the burgeoning merchant class. Twenty-four presses, over one hundred compositors, and a host of proofreaders, illuminators, and binders were in his employ. Due to this larger-scale operation, his shop was also among the first to separate the jobs of printing and selling books. In a modern sense, we would consider him a printer/publisher, since his products were often shipped to booksellers at other locations, instead of being sold directly from the printing shop.

Among the many famous works that issued from Koberger's press was the *Nuremberg Chronicle*, a pictorial history of the world from creation to 1490, compiled by Hartmann Schedel. The book comprised 645 woodcuts, some contributed by the famous engraver Albrecht Dürer. Its presence in the era of incunables is a reminder of how prominent xylography remained after moveable type was developed. The *Chronicle* was immensely popular and over 1,000 copies were printed in 1493, some in German and others in Latin. This marks one of the largest print runs of the incunable period.

Bookstores were appearing on every street in major cities between 1480 and 1500, as the flow of books off presses became a flood. Booksellers, unbridled from the task of printing, could focus their efforts on meeting consumer needs and enriching their inventory. One way to do this was to swap books with other booksellers, both locally and across great distances. A rich trade of books among retailers emerged, affording readers access to an array of authors and topics they would never have encountered previously.

Italian Printers

Fifteenth-century Italy, with the powerful papal states and the thriving republics of Florence and Venice, stood out as a vibrant commercial, political, and cultural hub in early-modern Europe. Venice, for example, was host to one of the largest industrial establishments of the time: the Venetian Arsenal. With over one thousand employees, the arsenal housed a full-time ship-building operation whose vessels, although controlled by the state, were used for privately funded trading efforts. The harbors of this "maritime republic" bustled with hundreds of daily arrivals and departures by ships headed to the Orient and northern Europe. The result of such nascent capitalist activity in cities throughout Italy was the emergence of a rich merchant society and a literate middle class. It is therefore not surprising that, after Germany, printing shops were established in Italian cities.

Venice, Rome, and Florence were among the benefactors of the Mainz diaspora, as printers from the north brought their fonts, presses, and aspirations to a society with a literate public whose demand for books was growing every day. The first press established in Italy was located in a Benedictine monastery near Rome. But it was Venice that quickly emerged as the center of the book trade in Italy. By 1470, there were at least fifty typographers at work in the city, most of them German (Redgrave 1894, 3).

Instrumental to Venetian emergence as a printing center were the efforts of three people: the brothers John and Wendelin da Spira (from Speier, a Rhenish city) and Nicolaus Jenson, all of whom learned their craft in Germany. John da Spira was granted a monopoly on official printing in 1467 by the Cabinet of Venice, a move that virtually assured his financial success. Two years later he produced Venice's first printed book: *Epistolae ad Familiares* (*Letters to Friends*), a work of the great Roman orator Cicero. Da Spira's major innovation in this book was the introduction of a type that broke from the Germanic Gothic type and offered more rounded letters, pleasing to the eye. This style of type would ultimately replace Gothic fonts throughout most of Europe. The 300 copies initially printed sold out in less than four months and another 300 were printed to meet the demand. The colophon to this pioneering work reflects da Spira's sense for his place in printing history: "For John, a man whom few in skill surpass / Has shown that books may best be writ with brass. Speier befriends Venice" (Steinberg 1959, 72).

Nicolaus Jenson (1420–1480) worked alongside da Spira and had an equally significant influence on the appearance of printed books. A Frenchman by birth, Jenson went to Germany in 1458 to be trained in the craft of printing or, as some would have it, to spy on the German printers for the king of France and return with their secrets. Whatever his motivations when he set out, he took advantage of his time in Mainz to learn the various aspects of the trade. His reputation as a prolific punch-cutter with a sense for aesthetically appealing type quickly grew. Following in da Spira's steps, Jenson produced a type—called roman—that readers found appealing. The way the individual letters fit together was less rigid than the *textur* of German books. His shop in Venice produced approximately 150 works between 1470 and 1480.

Print runs in this period rarely exceeded 500 copies, and most of these were still printed on vellum—a holdover from the manuscript days and an indication that the targeted audience for these books was manuscript collectors. But during Jenson's tenure in Venice, the craft of printing began to change, adopting a more business-like approach to the production of books. Jenson received the support of wealthy financial backers who provided supplies and much-needed capital. In return, they received a percentage of the profit from books sold. For this venture to be successful, the readership needed to expand, and here Jenson made just the right changes to the book to ensure that this expansion would happen.

Erhard Ratdolt, a printer from the German city of Augsburg, also relocated to Venice in 1476, where he made significant contributions to the technology of books. He was the first to use the decorated capital letters (called "flourishes") at the beginning of paragraphs, the first to include a title page where the printing house, date of publication, and city of publication were all identified, the first to include multicolored woodcuts, and the first to issue "type specimens"—pages that displayed the available types a print shop offered.

In 1476 Ratdolt printed his first book in Venice, the *Kalendarium*, for the famous German mathematician Johannes Müller (known by his Latin name, Regiomontanus). What is striking about this particular work is that it was issued both before and after the advent of the printing press, bridging this unique span in the history of the book. The work had been printed for Müller in Nuremberg using xylography, with the original images and text both carved in relief on wood. A series of thirty-one woodblocks printed back-to-back constituted the book. When Ratdolt printed the work with moveable metal type and separate engravings three years later, it was far more elegant production.

The skills, specialization, and commercial value embodied in the incunables is perhaps best seen in Ratdolt's 1482 edition of Euclid's classic work *The Elements of Geometry*, which was dedicated to the Doge of Venice. The book had 138 leaves (276 pages) and 420 woodcuts illustrating the Euclidean propositions. In addition to becoming the standard edition of Euclid throughout Europe, it earned Ratdolt a reputation as a specialist printer of scientific and mathematical works, the first of the period.

Typographically, the *Elements* advanced printing technology in several ways, utilizing special type for algebraic symbols and plates for geometric shapes. The book was also the first known to be printed simultaneously in multiple colors, which Ratdolt managed by breaking the different parts of the page into blocks that could be inked separately. Prior to this, a page would undergo one press for each color ink involved, resulting in two to three impressions on one page. Mathematical texts after Ratdolt's Euclid would be expected to provide such illustrations of problems. Finally, the book's dedication to the doge was printed with ink made from gold, an opulent technique that speaks to the wealth that was often underwriting such early printers.

With over 150 presses established in Venice during the incunable period, there were many more innovations and techniques than can be discussed here. But a look at catalogs of books for sale can provide some insight into the kinds of books Italian printers produced. Given that Italy was so firmly in the grip of the Catholic Church, it is somewhat surprising, perhaps, to find that the majority of Italian incunables were not religious texts. Thirty-five percent of the earliest books printed in Venice were classical texts, a fact that highlights the secularism unleashed by the Renaissance. Of the remaining, 20 percent were theological in nature, 17 percent dealt with law, 12 percent treated science, and 16 percent miscellaneous topics (King 2005, 266).

Costs of books also reveal their potential markets. Who could afford books in the incunable period when the print technology was fairly new? In Rome, around 1470, the price for an edition of the classical author Virgil was two ducats. St. Augustine's work *City of God* went for five ducats, while a Latin Bible cost ten ducats. According to a scholar who has examined sales records, a skilled artisan earned about three ducats in a month. Books, then, were not a casual purchase.

French Printers

German printers were invited to move to Paris in 1470 by professors and theologians from the Sorbonne, the famous Paris university. The result of this academic patronage was twofold. First, the printers found a captive audience among students who needed a steady supply of philosophical, legal, and theological textbooks. The clerics who ran the Sorbonne also demanded ecclesiastical books. But this dynamic of academic patronage led to constraints, as printers were much less free in their selection of book topics. Their work was highly regulated by university officials, and, unlike printers in Italy who had license to print a wide range of material, the Parisian publishers suffered restrictions—both topical and aesthetic—from their customers.

One of the most commonly printed books in Paris during this period was the *Book of Hours*, a famous prayer book dating from the late fifteenth century. Originally used by monks to keep track of the daily prayer cycle, the printed *Book of Hours* was smaller and more amenable to use by an individual. Its calendar helped individuals keep track of religious feasts and festivals, important religious days and their attendant prayers, and passages of scripture. Not only practical, the book was beautifully illustrated with forty-nine woodcuts depicting Old Testament scenes. The *Book of Hours* was sought after by readers across the social spectrum. Even households where few members were literate might have had a family copy of this book. Of all the incunables issued from French presses, few match the artistry of these works. They combined the practical—an affordable, consistent guide to religious practice—with the aesthetic, each book an artistic statement.

At the close of the fifteenth century there were approximately sixty printers in Paris. This number was rivaled by the forty presses in Lyon, a city in the south of France that emerged as a hub of early printing activity. Without the controlling hand of the Sorbonne, printers in Lyon enjoyed a great deal of freedom and produced many works influenced by the humanist movement of Italy. They also printed numerous works in the vernacular, treating such practical topics as husbandry and health, as well as more whimsical issues like romance. Even the famous German printer Anton Koberger had a branch of his print shop in Lyon, testimony to the city's international flavor.

English Printers

Unlike France and Italy, the printed book's path to England was circuitous, with the first books printed in the English language appearing on the Continent. William Caxton, an advisor to the English Royal family, went to Cologne in 1471 to learn the techniques of printing from Ulrich Zell, a Mainz priest. By 1475 Caxton was living in Bruges (in present-day Belgium) and had both translated and printed *The Recuyell of the Historyes of Troye*, a well-known French romance. In the colophon to that book, Caxton complained of the difficulty he had writing out long passages, "myn hand wery and not stedfast, myn eyen dimmed with overmoche lokyng on the whit paper," but, he says:

> I have practysed and lerned at my great charge and dispense to ordeyne this said book in prynte after the manner and form as ye may here see, and is not wreton with penne and ynke, as other bokes [sic] ben . . . for all the bookes [sic] of this storye named the Recule of the Historyes of Troyes thus enprynted as ye here see, were begonne in oon day and also fyysshid in oon day. (Berry and Poole 1966, 34)

Caxton's second work, *The Game and Playe of the Chesse* appeared in 1474 and is a good example of how quickly books expanded in their scope. Books about games, dancing, cooking, and hunting earned printers new audiences.

In 1476 Caxton returned to his native England and established a print shop beneath the sign of the Red Pale, near Westminster Abbey in London. It would not be long before dozens of signs hanging outside printing houses would display their respective printer's devices, the emblems found in the colophons of their books. The first book Caxton printed in England was entitled *Dictes or Sayengis of the Philosophers*. Written by Edward IV's brother-in-law, Caxton no doubt received a good commission to see it into print. Indeed, though he produced popular works that middle-class readers purchased, his success was still largely dependent upon royal patronage.

Ultimately, Caxton's printing house produced over ninety books, seventy-four of which were in English. Many of these he translated himself. England was the first place to commonly print books in its own language, a trend that would soon catch on in other regions of Europe. However, the style of type that was fashionable in the kingdom—a cursive variant of Gothic type, known as *bâtarde*—was not widely adopted outside England.

Dutch Printers

Though the Germans hold a preeminent place in the history of printed books, the Dutch have long maintained that moveable type is their own innovation. It was not Gutenberg, the Dutch assert, but a man by the name of Coster who first developed the idea of metal type that could produce multiple impressions. Historians have explored this dispute from every angle, concluding that the Dutch claims to priority are, at a minimum, unprovable, and must be considered with skepticism.

The first printed book that can firmly be attributed to a printer in the Low Countries (what we consider Holland today) appeared in 1473 in the city of Utrecht. In the age of incunables, other Dutch cities such as Delft and Gouda also opened printing shops, but it would not be until the sixteenth and seventeenth centuries—Holland's golden age—that Holland would become home to some of the world's finest printers.

Iberian Printing

The history of printing in Spain is intimately connected to its tradition of conquest. Having been occupied by the Moors (Muslims) since the eighth century, the Spanish Crown embarked on a "Reconquest" (*reconquista*) from the eleventh through the thirteenth centuries. In the midst of this military effort, Spanish writers devoted themselves to tales of religiously inspired nobles and valiant warriors, all of whom were cast in romantic terms. The Catholic Church was a major patron of the books produced, but surprisingly, the books printed were not predominantly ecclesiastical in nature.

When the printing press arrived in 1474, there was a body of romantic and religious literature that printers were eager to distribute more widely. The city of Valencia in Aragon was the first to establish a press. A German company called "The Great Trading Company of Ravensburg" (which had offices in Spain, Italy, Flanders, France, Poland, and Hungary) dispatched three printers to Valencia to set up shop, making Spain yet another beneficiary of German printing experience. Despite the foreign seed, printed books in Spain quickly developed into a uniquely Hispanic style. They were often printed in the vernacular using a slightly rounded Gothic type called *rotunda*. Roman type had been introduced, but was rejected by Spaniards, who preferred a more rigid type that mimicked the handwriting of Iberian scribes.

Not surprisingly, when the Spanish did establish an empire in the Americas, they would export the printing press across the Atlantic. First Mexico, and then cities in South America established their own printing houses, about which more will be said in the next chapter.

In the Cradle No Longer

On the eve of the sixteenth century, the technology, both of the book itself and of the means of printing it, had spread from its birthplace in Mainz to every major European city. Books had diversified in myriad ways. New authors, new topics, new sizes, and new fonts were introduced within a generation of Gutenberg. With these came increasing print runs,

and the craftsmanship that made an incunable book so similar to its manuscript ancestor quickly diminished. By the early sixteenth century, quantity
would replace quality as readers increased in number, and the demand
placed on printing houses precluded the possibility of small tended print
runs with hand illuminations. Indeed, it was this demand for more books
that led printers to streamline their methods.

Book production quickly became a series of specialized tasks carried
out with increasing efficiency. Specialist compositors worked for printing
houses that focused on specific kinds of text, while the tasks of papermaking, typecasting, editing, and binding were farmed out to experts in the respective areas. While this led to a slight homogenization in the appearance
of printed books, it also forced the technology of books to evolve in new
and interesting ways. If the latter half of the fifteenth century saw books in
their infancy, the sixteenth century would prove to be a period of exciting
maturation: the youthful century of printed books.

3

Youth: Books in the Sixteenth Century

BOOKS AND SOCIETY: A PROTEST IN PRINT

The sixteenth century was a period of sweeping change in Europe. The cultural and intellectual ferment of the late Renaissance opened the doors for the religious upheaval of the Reformation, precipitated widespread economic growth, and stimulated momentous advances in science and technology. It was a rich and exciting period for many Europeans. It was also a time that was ripe for the development of quicker, more efficient means of communication. With the printing press widely distributed, and its use increasing, new techniques in papermaking, typecasting, and bookbinding emerged. Readers demanded increasingly diverse material for their collections, and printers responded with an ever-widening array of topics—including histories of the printing press. This chapter examines the technology of the book in this rich historical context and surveys the major aesthetic and technical innovations in book production that emerged in the sixteenth century.

As recent historians, such as Lisa Jardine, have shown, the driving force behind the book market was an exploding demand for access to information. Printers, poised to exploit this demand, were among a group of relative newcomers to the European scene: entrepreneurially minded capitalists, a class found only rarely before the Renaissance. It is no accident that the first presses were established in Europe's great commercial centers—Venice, Antwerp, Lyon, and Frankfurt.

The exponentially increasing demand for books points to a growing literate audience: educated men—and in some cases women—who had adopted the ideals of Renaissance humanism and sought books to fulfill their needs. Some were historians, some were philologists (humanist scholars trained to study the use of language), while many others were simply intellectuals, eager to explore the works of the ancients in order to refine their education and broaden their knowledge. In the atmosphere of sixteenth-century Europe, the number of such intellectuals grew, and not just among wealthy aristocrats. Middle-class bankers and merchants sought out and purchased books for their collections. In some cases, the books were read for pleasure: poetry, romances, histories, and travel books. Others were related to a businessman's field, such as Jan Christoffels's 1547 work *A notable and very excellente worke expressing and declaring the maner and forme how to keep a book of accounts or reconings*. Another was William Carter's *England's Glory: By the benefit of wool manufactured therein, from the farmer to the merchant*. There were also books geared toward social values, exemplified by the work *Dialogues and advice for women, to provide them with virtuosity and happiness*, written in 1583 by a group of Frenchmen. Meeting with this growing demand were specialty presses, some known for the quality of their work, others for their lower costs.

The appearance of books changed significantly from the incunable era, largely for reasons of economy. But changes in books were also motivated by the religious, political, and cultural tumult of the late Renaissance. Initially collector's items, books became mass-produced commodities, printed in numbers that vastly exceeded the total number of volumes—both manuscript and print—that had existed on the eve of the century. The numbers alone are sufficient testimony. In the middle of the incunable period—around 1480—there were approximately 100 printing establishments in Europe. By 1500, there were 1,100 shops in over 260 cities (Chappell 1999, chap. 5). In Paris alone, in 1550, there were 332 books printed, compared to just 88 books in 1501, nearly a fourfold increase (Febvre and Martin 1990, 264).

Printing in the Reformation

While secular works were increasingly common in the sixteenth century, they were printed alongside—not in lieu of—religious books, whose production increased dramatically with the arrival of the Reformation. Since the time of St. Peter, the Catholic Church had been *the* Church in Europe. Internal strife, however, led to a split—or schism—in the eleventh century and the church divided into two: the Roman Catholic Church in the west (what we think of as Europe) and the Orthodox Church in the east (what was called Byzantium). The theological reasons behind the schism are too complex to explore here, but it was the Catholic Church—under the guidance of the Pope—that retained its preeminent position as the religion of the Latin west.

The church's role, however, was far more than just religious in this period. It was equally political and economic. From its founding, it was the primary institution that held society together. As Christ's representative on Earth, the Pope ranked above all local monarchs, and from the papal offices in Rome to the smallest parish in the French countryside, the mandates of the church were heeded by its parishioners. The rhythms of peoples' lives were influenced by the church through prayer, Mass, and holy days, and the hope of salvation provided all the motivation the faithful needed to obey church instructions. It also provided the impetus for tithing, making the church the wealthiest and the most powerful institution in the western world. All this until the Reformation.

In the early sixteenth century, a number of individuals began speaking out against what they considered egregious abuses on the part of the church, including the practice of issuing "indulgences." Parishioners and members of the laity had long been allowed to give money to the church as a way of paying for their sins or, in some cases, reducing the amount of time they would have to spend in purgatory after death. On purchasing the indulgence, the sinner would get a slip of paper from a priest, verifying that a certain amount had been paid and a certain level of sin absolved. Once the printing press was developed, the church was able to print indulgences at a record pace, greatly expanding the scope of the practice. People could purchase unlimited indulgences for themselves and for loved ones (including those who had already died). By the sixteenth century, the sale of indulgences was bringing in enormous sums of money to the Pope in Rome, but some clerics found the practice unconscionable, and demanded that it be eliminated.

Most famous among these reformers was Martin Luther, an Augustinian monk with a humanistic background who taught at the university in Wittenberg (present-day Germany). In 1517, Luther posted ninety-five theses—or complaints—against the Catholic Church on the door of his local rectory. Though the act of posting theological positions was a standard mode of debate in Luther's academic environment, his indictment of the church went far beyond intellectual wordplay. The moment was ripe. Catholic fiscal abuses were rampant, and Luther's arguments resonated loudly and spread quickly throughout Europe.

The response from the Catholic Church, which recognized at once the threat of this doctrinal debate, was to launch a Counter-Reformation: a wholesale effort to reform the most corrupt aspects of the church while trying to reign in on—and in some cases severely punish—detractors. Luther was excommunicated, and his arguments countered by the church with their own propaganda. Their pace, however, hardly matched his. Luther's little booklets (known as *Flügschriften* in German, or "flying writings") outnumbered the Catholic Church's publications by five against one (Edwards 1994, 29). Cheaply printed, often in the vernacular, and easily carried or shipped, the printed booklets flooded cities such as Augsburg, Nuremberg, and Wittenberg. The most dominant and cohesive institution in sixteenth-century life, the Catholic Church, faced a more serious threat than the Islamic advance at its greatest, all thanks to printed books.

In one of history's great ironies, the very printing press that allowed the church to abuse its authority through the printing of indulgences was the instrument that enabled Luther's dissent to be so quickly reproduced and so widely read. Without the press, the Reformation would scarcely have risen above the level of local quarrels. But by utilizing the technology of printed books, Luther and his peers rapidly disseminated their ideas and changed the demographics of theological debate. Their defiance of Catholic doctrine was made accessible to numerous readers through large print runs: between 1500 and 1530, an estimated 10,000 booklets were printed. His "Sermon on Indulgences and Grace," given in 1517, was printed and distributed to every major city in the Holy Roman Empire. The fact that the book was written in German only hastened its reception by the laity, who could not read the Latin in which most clerical documents were written.

While the theological contest intensified, and the church found itself pitted against a major voice of dissent, printing houses lined up for the book and pamphlet contracts that would come their way from either side. In some areas, print shops earned reputations for being sympathetic to the reformers, or Protestants. In Catholic regions, such as France and Italy, presses were eager to take on the lucrative tasks of printing missals and church edicts. The printed book, less than a century after its inception, was universally recognized as the most efficient messenger for disseminating religious doctrine.

Luther's criticisms against the Catholic Church targeted not only their corrupt economic practices, but their monopoly on scriptural interpretation as well. He protested that parishioners had no real understanding of the Mass since it was read to them in Latin, which few could comprehend.

Luther's answer to this was to translate the scripture into German, and then have it printed and distributed, thus allowing people to consider it for themselves. His version of the New Testament—one of the most important books of the sixteenth century—emerged from the Wittenberg press of Melchoir Lotther in 1522. The first print run of over 3,000 copies sold out within two months, and a second edition was immediately printed. Between 1522 and 1525, at least 86,000 copies of the Lutheran Bible were printed (Edwards 1994, 123). Though expensive—costing anywhere from two weeks to two months' salary for the average worker—Luther's New Testament reflected the power and influence of the printed word.

Luther's vernacular Bible was intended for a new crop of readers, a crop harvested outside the institutional margins of the Catholic Church. This shift in readership prompted him to include a preface in his New Testament that would serve as a guide to the book's contents:

> necessity demands a notice and prefaces to be placed [in this book] so that the simple person will be led from his old delusion on to the right way and instructed in what he should expect in this book so that he not seek commandments and laws where he should be seeking Gospel and the promises of God. (Edwards 1994, 111)

Not all sixteenth-century books were dedicated to the prosecution of Reformation debates, but the stimulus that Luther and his peers provided to book production is undeniable. Books were printed quickly, cheaply, and in a range of styles that would have proven an impossibility to incunable printers.

DIVERSITY IN THE FAMILY: NEW FORMATS, NEW TOPICS

Books printed between 1450 and 1500 retained the characteristics of their predecessor manuscript books, even as they applied the new technology of moveable type. They were transitional objects, not only reflecting the craftsmanship of an earlier age but also foreshadowing the mass-produced, market-oriented printing business that would eventually morph into something recognizable as the modern world of publishing. In the sixteenth century, demand for books grew exponentially, and the book evolved in lockstep with this growth in demand. The way books looked, felt, and were read were all changing. Inside and out, the printed book of the sixteenth century was a technology in a state of rapid advance.

New Types

Back to Gutenberg: the type of his forty-two-line Bible intentionally resembled the manuscript "hand" of German monks. But within fifty years of this work, the attractiveness of scribal handwriting gave way to the clarity of more utilitarian scripts, as earlier chapters have shown. The popularity of Gothic type was soon rivaled by a rounder type known as *antiqua*. During the Italian Renaissance, humanists had developed a script that was distinctly different from that used elsewhere in Europe. As scholars of the late fourteenth and early fifteenth centuries copied and commented on the works of the ancients—Cicero, Livy, and Horace—they did so in a clear and elegant handwriting known, appropriately, as *lettera antiqua*. The letters were less jagged than Gothic letters, and the appearance of the handwriting was generally more rounded. Both Gothic and antiqua evolved several subtypes—for example, Fraktur and Schwabacher were Gothic types—and more were on the way, as books changed shape and size and consumers demanded greater readability.

Francesco Petrarch, the great Renaissance humanist introduced in Chapter 1, is among those who found the Gothic handwriting of northern Europe to be aesthetically displeasing, much as Italians generally disliked the harsh appearance of Gothic architecture. Gothic script, Petrarch said, "tired the eyes" and in its place he preferred a variant called *rotunda*. Also known as Italian Gothic, the letters of this script were rounded, bigger, and separated from each other on the page. The result was a more aesthetically appealing type that harkened back to the clean, clear letters used on the buildings of ancient Rome. This "humanist script" was widely used throughout Italy during the Renaissance and it was the reason Italian printers were so eager to locate an alternative to the German Gothic fonts.

Ironically, the alternative they found—called roman type—was the product of a German typemaker. Created in 1467, roman fonts resembled the humanist script used in Italy. They were rejected by German printers in favor of traditional Gothic fonts, but in Venice, they had an enthusiastic reception. Printers like Nicolaus Jenson adopted roman type in the 1470s and it quickly became the hallmark of early Italian printing. By the mid-sixteenth century, roman type was being used by printers in France, the Low Countries, and England.

Shortly after the introduction of roman type, the famous Italian printer Aldus Manutius introduced books printed with slanted and more compact letters. Known as italic, it was a close cousin to the roman letters, and both roman and italic were eventually subsumed under the general heading of antiqua fonts. Manutius used his italic type to print works in both Latin and

Greek, the latter requiring that all new characters be cast. By the late fifteenth century, he had printed the complete works of Aristotle in the original Greek, testimony to the audience that existed at the time for classical works. Renaissance scholars hoped to recover the wisdom of the ancients, and Manutius supplied them with the tools to do so.

In 1501, Manutius printed an edition of Virgil's *Opera*, the collected works of the great Roman poet. Every two months for the next five years, Manutius produced classical works in what became a famous series of pocket books known as "Aldine" editions, after their printer. The condensed size of italic type had several implications for both the printer and the reader. First, the smaller type meant that the page size could be reduced. Smaller pages meant smaller books, cheaper to print and more accessible to book buyers with limited funds. Second, demand for the Aldine editions translated into larger print runs, and further economies of scale. Prior to Manutius's time, books were normally printed in small runs of 100 to 250 books. Manutius's press issued print runs of 1,000 books at a time—nothing compared to the run of a current best-seller, but still testimony to the increased readership that awaited these first popular books.

Italian printer Aldus Manutius in his shop. Courtesy of the Library of Congress.

Third, the compact size of the Aldine editions and their descendants allowed readers to carry them easily, a stark contrast to the days when 20-pound books were chained to immovable wooden desks. The Aldines did for books what laptops did for computers in the twentieth century. Scholarship became mobile and reading was no longer an activity confined to the study.

The only downside of these editions was the relative manageability of reading the italic. Though not as troublesome as Gothic, the letters were still hard to read, and this eventually tempered enthusiasm for these little books. But the use of roman type grew more and more popular, and typecasters developed innumerable variants on its clean appearance. Over time, many more roman types would be developed, some with longer axes, others with alterations to the individual parts of a letter—called ascenders and descenders. Though the variations are many, roman type eventually dominated the world of print and remains the font with which we are most familiar and comfortable.

Type-designers

As roman type grew in popularity, printers were eager to procure the highest quality sorts possible. Whereas fifteenth-century printers were typically responsible for casting their own type, the craft became more specialized after the incunable period. Men like Claude Garamond (1480–1561) and Robert Granjon (1513–1589), both from France, earned reputations as master type-designers. Their high-quality punches and matrices were sought after by printers everywhere. Garamond developed an elegant roman type—inspired by types of Manutius and Jenson—that printers found highly desirable. Indeed, the Garamond font remains one of the most popular modern fonts. For his part, Robert Granjon focused on italic types and in particular, a type called *Civilité*, which was sold to the major printing shops in Europe at the time.

The result of this specialization in typecasting was uniformity. In the earliest stages of print technology, each printing house had cast its own type, giving each shop a unique "hand." The advent of expert type-designers meant that a printer in Antwerp and a printer in Venice could easily be using type cast by the same craftsman. Whether this homogenization of type was to the reader's advantage is debatable, but it was certainly welcomed by printers who sought to reproduce famous editions of a work at a profit—an early example of the piracy we associate today with videos, CDs, and DVDs.

In the sixteenth century, the notion of copyright was not defined. The result was that a printer could purchase a copy of a book (or else gain access to it surreptitiously by paying off a compositor for stolen galley proofs) and then set the type for it in his own shop and begin selling copies. These pirated copies were often of a lesser quality than the original, but they were cheaper and would quickly saturate the market, making money for the pirate printer and undercutting any profit the original printer hoped to make. As types became uniform, this bootleg operation became easier, and printers had to be wary of who worked in their shops. At least, they hoped to prevent pirated books from appearing before the original copies, so that they would have a chance to recoup the investment.

Book Formats: Variation in Sizes

As type size changed, so did the size of books. The Bible that emerged from Gutenberg's press in the 1450s was printed in "folio," which means that one large piece of paper—over a foot tall—was folded in half to produce two leaves, or four pages. Books printed in folio tended to be elaborate, since they used a significant amount of paper. As economy became a priority, printers sought ways to reduce the amount of paper. By casting smaller type, they could fit more text on a page, but a large page filled with small type was difficult to read and cumbersome to carry around.

The answer to this problem was to print on smaller sheets of paper. Folding the paper in half twice created four leaves (eight pages); this format is referred to as "quarto" and quickly became an accepted standard. In the same vein, paper could be folded three times, creating eight leaves (sixteen pages). This is called printing in "octavo." The pattern continues, with books becoming increasingly small: in the "duodecimo" (12mo) format, paper is folded into twelve leaves to yield twenty-four pages , and so forth up to the wholly unreadable 64mo. Today, museums and rare-book libraries exhibit miniature books that exemplify these rare formats. The record holder is a leather-bound book measuring 2.4×2.9 mm: almost exactly the same size as the head on a match with text that is actually legible if viewed through a magnifying glass. Generally speaking, however, quarto and octavo were the most commonly printed formats in the sixteenth century.

These formats presented the printer with a challenge: how to print several pages of type on a single sheet of paper that will end up being folded multiple times. In the simplest case—a folio book—the leaf would receive just two impressions (one on each side) and the sheet of paper (two leaves) would be folded down the middle, like a standard greeting card today. But for a book printed in quarto, the sheet would receive four impressions per side, each oriented sideways so that it could be properly read after the paper was folded twice and the edges cut to separate the leaves. The process became increasingly complex with each new fold in the paper.

To ensure that the pages were right-way up after the folds were cut, printers used "signatures," an early form of pagination. Each large piece of paper—no matter how many individual pages printed on it—was assigned a letter of the alphabet. The first impression for a quarto book was labeled A, and the individual leaves stamped on it marked A_1, A_2, A_3, A_4. These signatures guided the printer as he did his work, and with each newly printed paper, the letter changed. The first "gathering" for a quarto book would be A_1–A_4, the second B_1–B_4, etc. In an octavo book, the signatures would go from A_1–A_8. When all the gatherings had been printed and cut, they were sewn together to make the book.

Signatures were one tool printers used to keep the pages and gatherings in order. Tag-words were another. At the bottom corner of each right-

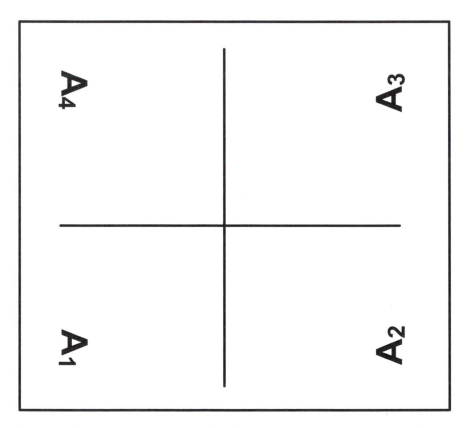

The layout for a quarto page, arranged so that four impressions can be made. Once printed, the page will be folded twice, making four leaves, or eight pages.

hand page, the first letters of the following page were printed. These catch-words guided the printer in his assembly of the gatherings, assuring him that the pages were in the proper order.

Ultimately, both signatures and catchwords were replaced in the six-teenth century by page numbers that ran throughout the book. Pagination not only made it easier for readers to reference specific parts of a book, but also led to the introduction of an index, a welcome tool for readers to lo-cate specific parts of a book without reading it in its entirety.

Front Matter

Leading up to the text of a modern book are a number of preliminary pages referred to in the publishing trade as "front matter." Included in this material (though not necessarily present in every book) are the title page, frontispiece—a full-page illustration related to the book's theme—a dedi-cation, table of contents, list of illustrations, foreword, preface, and acknowl-edgments. Sometimes the introduction is considered front matter as well. Because these parts of the book sit outside the actual text, they are collec-tively referred to as "paratext." But their appearance at the front of a book as not immediate, just as indices and endnotes did not appear at the back of early books.

The book you are presently reading has its title page on a right-hand page, called the "recto." Indeed, almost every title page today is placed on the right side. This page provides the reader with the most basic of intro-ductions: here is the name of the book and its creator, or author. Addition-ally, the title page identifies the publisher—the book's house of origin—and the date of publication. Flip the title page over and on the next left-hand page, called the "verso," are additional details, typically in smaller type. These include copyright date, reprint and translation references, ISBN number, and perhaps information about the book's type and method of printing. This wealth of information, however, was neither available nor necessary in the age of manuscripts. A book written or copied by a scribe was almost always bound without any identifier of its contents on the pages. At best, the book's title was on the spine of the binding. When one opened the book, text simply began on the first visible page. Occasionally, one might find a scribe's signature—in a form similar to later printed colophons—on the back page, but the use of a title page was deemed unnecessary and (given the expense of vellum and paper) quite wasteful. This changed with the printing press. Toward the end of the incunable period, printers generally adopted the custom of including a title page, for practical and aesthetic reasons.

Unlike books in the manuscript era, those from the printing press were rarely bound. Instead, printing houses stocked unbound copies, leaving the binding up to the purchaser's taste. Unbound copies of books were also easier and cheaper for booksellers to trade with each other—especially when shipping over great distances was involved. The problem was that the first and the last page of the book were exposed and therefore easily torn or stained. To remedy this, printers started protecting the first page of text with a cover sheet and it only made sense to have the book's title clearly printed on it.

Initially, title pages contained just that—the book's title. Any other information was relegated to the colophon, which continued to be printed below the last line of text. But slowly, the amount of information in the colophon outgrew the amount of blank space printers had after the last line of a book. This information was slowly moved to the book's front. What started as a fairly straightforward cover sheet—the basic title page—evolved into a decorative page detailing the book's title, author, printer, publisher, and both the date and city of its publication. Ornamental borders were also added, framing this information in intricate floral or geometric patterns. Ultimately, the title page became one of the book's most crowded pages—sometimes to the point of distraction. Not until the eighteenth century did printers move away from this style, returning to a more modest title page.

Printer's Devices

As the market for printed books grew in the fifteenth century, printers began using unique insignias, known as devices, to mark their involvement in a book's creation. Johann Fust and Peter Schöffer used the first known device in a printed book in the colophon of their 1457 *Psalter*. Soon, the practice was ubiquitous. Printers used marks of their own or adopted one of several famous motifs for their device. Aldus Manutius first used his device—an anchor with a dolphin wrapping around it—in 1502.

Much as a surname and a crest connects all the distant relatives of a family, the printer's mark linked books that were topically and aesthetically different from one another. Such devices were only rarely found in manuscripts. The prevalence of the device or emblem signaled the printer's need to claim credit for his work. This was particularly important for those printers who produced especially high-quality or otherwise exceptional books.

As books became increasingly commodified, a printer with a reputation for craftsmanship (i.e., good paper or fine inks) could be recognized by his device and therefore could sell more books. It was essentially a marketing effort in an age when the idea of marketing was not yet fully articulated. And so successful was the device in selling books that some presses would consciously adopt a device that looked suspiciously like the device of a reputable press. Given the lack of copyright laws in the fifteenth and sixteenth centuries, there was little that could be done about the practice.

Print shops commonly displayed their device on their sign, which hung outside the shop doors. "Printed at the sign of the ————" was a phrase one might have read in a book, reflecting both printing house and address.

Illustrations

The aesthetic appeal and informational utility of illustrations and diagrams antedated the age of print. We have examined the work of illuminators, who were responsible for creating many of the images in manuscript books, but such labor-intensive methods obviously could not keep pace with the hundreds of books capable of being churned out by a printing press in one day. As the technology of the printed book evolved, so did the ability of printers and artists to produce elegant and beautiful illustrations.

As mentioned earlier, illustrations were added to books by means of woodcuts. In this technique, images were produced in a block of hardwood—such as apple or beech—in relief and in reverse. After the introduction of moveable type, woodcuts were in even greater demand. In 1460, Albrecht Pfister—using type created by Johann Fust—printed the first book with woodcut illustrations. In 1471, he printed *The Jewel* by Ulrich Boner, a collection of fairy tales that included over one hundred hand-colored images. Because the woodcut and the type were not the same height, a page with illustrations initially required Pfister to make two sequential impressions, but by 1480, text and image could be printed simultaneously.

By the fifteenth century, French, Italian, and English woodcutters were contributing to handsome volumes of natural history, astronomy, classics, and, of course, biblical works. Among the many products of the woodcut era, two stand out as exceptional. The first is the 1493 *Liber Chronicarum* or *Nuremberg Chronicle* printed by Anton Koberger (see Chapter 2). The *Chronicle* included 1,809 illustrations, including 596 images of popes and royalty. Despite this number of personal images, only seventy-two woodcuts were used, meaning that the same woodcut was used to represent multiple individuals, with only a change in the caption identifying the person. Creating over 500 woodcuts, one for each emperor or pope, was hardly pragmatic, so the categorization of images (with, for example, one or two woodcuts serving as images for all popes) was an efficient way to illustrate a book. The practice also exemplifies the rather loose association between image and text in early illustrations. A printer had a limited supply of woodcuts on hand and was often forced to use an image that did not directly deal with the text on that page. For example, a Bible printed in 1572 actually is illustrated with images from Greek mythology (Steinberg 1959, 158). Woodcuts, then, were widely adopted by the sixteenth century, but their artistry often remained disconnected from the author's text.

The famous German engraver Albrecht Dürer produced fifteen woodcuts for his work *Apocalypse* (1498). These images display an unrivaled level of craftsmanship, and represent what is possibly the high point of woodcutting art. Their style, naturalistic and realistic, clearly reflects a Renaissance influence.

Dürer's work also serves as an example of specialization in woodcutting. While he was renowned as a draftsman and produced sketches of the highest quality, he was often not responsible for the fabrication of the woodcut itself. Instead, Dürer would draw the image on the wood and leave the cutting to an apprentice, albeit a very accomplished one. Because the craft was regulated by a guild system, apprentices such as Dürer's achieved a high level of proficiency before they were taken on for major illustrating projects. There was artistry, then, both in the sketch and in the actual cutting of the wood.

The first alternative to the woodcut was the copperplate engraving, which arrived on the printing scene around 1477. Whereas a woodcut image was created in relief, a copperplate engraving had the image actually carved into the surface, in what is called intaglio, after the Italian word *tagliare*, meaning "to carve." To generate an image on copper, an engraver first drew the image in reverse on a piece of paper. This paper was then set on top of a metal plate, typically copper, which had a wax coating on it. By tracing over the drawing with a sharp tool, the image was impressed onto the wax surface, though the copper beneath it would still be untouched. Finally, the paper was removed and a tool called a graver retraced the lines of the image, cutting through the wax and digging in to the metal plate.

What the artist had originally drawn on the sheet of paper now existed as a recessed image on a copper plate. The next step was to ink the copperplate, and then wipe the surface clear, so that the only ink remaining was in the recesses of the carved lines. A piece of damp paper was then placed over this plate and both the paper and the copperplate were sent through a special press, which applied enough pressure to transfer the ink to the paper.

While this method of illustrating books allowed for sharper images, it was not nearly as popular as the woodcut method. The difficulty was that copperplates utilized intaglio printing while the type was in relief. One

One of sixteen woodcuts from Albrecht Dürer's *Apocalypse* series, published in Nuremberg, beginning in 1498. Courtesy of the Library of Congress.

surface was recessed while the other stood out. To use them simultaneously was difficult. Woodcuts, on the other hand, were created in the same way as type—in relief—and could therefore be printed at the same time as the text.

Because of this difference, printers began using copperplate engravings just for their title pages, while relying on woodcuts for the book's illustrations. They realized that a decorative border, their printer's device, and the book's title itself could be beautifully produced from a copper engraving, with its fine degrees of shading and detail. Not until the late seventeenth century would copperplate engravings be more extensively used throughout a book.

Bindings

As illustrations complemented and enhanced a book's interior, bindings added an element of artistry to the book's exterior. The business of binding books had always been separate from the creation of pages. In the days of manuscript, binderies were often in a building adjacent to the scriptorium or monastery. The crafts were clearly distinct. In the sixteenth century, with the production of printed books increasing exponentially, the task of binding had to be expedited as well.

Expensive volumes intended for select audiences called for craftsmanship that mimicked the bindings of the manuscript era. Such books were bound in silk, velvet, or leather and decorated with stamps, jewels, or gold leaf. For more popular editions, however, only a simple binding was needed. Calfskin and sheepskin were commonly used, and the title of the work was added to the spine. Sometimes this was written by hand, with a permanent ink; other times it was stamped onto the spine. By the sixteenth century, cardboard had replaced the wooden boards used in medieval bindings. The cardboard material was fabricated from layers of waste paper glued together to an appropriate thickness. Scholars studying the works of a particular press would frequently examine the scrap paper contained in deteriorating bindings, looking for insights into the workings of these early presses. Valuable galley proofs of famous texts are occasionally uncovered by a fortunate historian who, dissecting an early book cover, uncovers the "gold" in material that an early print shop considered "waste."

New Topics: Beyond the Religious Book

The pioneering books of Gutenberg, Fust, and their immediate successors were principally classical or theological works. By the sixteenth century, however, there was already significant expansion in the range of topics treated by printed books. A census of printed books in Strasbourg between 1515 and 1548 shows that 30 percent were Protestant texts, 16 percent scientific, 11 percent humanistic, 10 percent Bibles or biblical commentary, while 8 percent were expressly Catholic texts. The remaining books treated topics of local interest, law, and school subjects.

The earliest books dealing with scientific subjects are a good illustration of the revolutionary power of the new technology. Some of the most important works in the history of science were written and printed in the sixteenth century, during the period often called "the scientific revolution." The astronomer Nicolaus Copernicus published his book *On the Revolution of Heavenly Spheres* in 1543, suggesting that the Earth was not the center of the universe, but instead revolved around the Sun. This was a major cosmological shift and Copernicus's book—though admittedly written for trained astronomers and mathematicians—had a significant impact because many scholars could examine the book simultaneously, discussing it with each other and referring to it as a standardized text. At least 400 copies were printed and circulated, far more than would have been possible in a manuscript form.

In the same year, Andreas Vesalius—a physician and anatomist from Brussels—published *On the Fabric of the Human Body*, a comprehensive and beautifully illustrated anatomical work that revolutionized the study of the human body. The successive generations of students who studied this book added tremendously to the understanding of human anatomy and physiology. What made it so effective were the detailed illustrations of the skeletal, vascular, and muscular systems, each a woodcut (carved on pear wood) that provided the reader multiple perspectives on a given anatomical part. Vesalius's book, one historian wrote, marked "a defining moment in the history of illustration, and of anatomical illustration in particular, for it integrates the visual into the whole argument of the book. Both image and text are indispensable" (Nutton 2003, 18). What Vesalius accomplished in this book would have been unthinkable in the manuscript age, and the profound effects of his work reflect the powerful impact of the printed book on intellectual life.

In her famous work on print culture, historian Elizabeth Eisenstein examined the way that printed books affected critical events in the fifteenth and sixteenth centuries, including the scientific revolution of which Copernicus and Vesalius were an integral part. In comparing the eras of manuscripts and printed books, she identified key characteristics of print culture which allowed for ideas—be they about classical literature, scriptural interpretation, or the structure of the heavens—to be widely shared and explored. For scientific works in particular, Eisenstein demonstrated

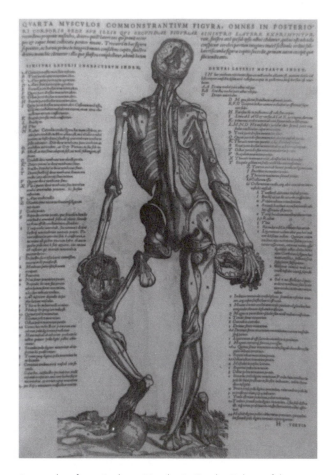

A woodcut from Andreas Vesalius's *On the Fabric of the Human Body*, published in 1543. This detailed and richly illustrated anatomical work had a tremendous influence on the practice of anatomy. Courtesy of the Library of Congress.

the various ways that printed books about astronomy, mathematics, and natural history opened the door to more fruitful analysis.

At the most basic level, the press rendered books more stable: errors were not multiplied with each subsequent copy. In the days of handwritten letters and manuscripts (which were duplicated tens or hundreds of times over), mistakes were invariably introduced and images, drawn by hand, varied in their accuracy. For a book depicting human or plant anatomy, such variations, however slight, had a significant impact on the accuracy with which a specimen was understood. With print, however, the text was "fixed," each copy from a given print run was identical. Of course, errors could be introduced by illustrators (woodcutters) or the compositors, but even those could be remedied partway through the printing process or in a later print run. The fixity of text, Eisenstein showed, meant that 500 copies of a work could be available immediately and those copies would be free from many of the errors that would have been made in the manuscript days.

What was true for scientific books held equally for books in the humanities, and as Lisa Jardine succinctly puts it, "By the 1520s, the partnership between book production and scholarship had become a merger" (1996, 227). With printed books, scholars could enjoy the luxury of owning and comparing different editions of the classics. Scholarship moved out of the realm of the wealthy, as scholars took advantage of cheaper, more portable books. The Aldine editions in particular were valued for their convenient size and faithfulness to the original texts. Manutius went to great lengths to ensure that the editions of Plato and Aristotle he printed were the most accurate versions of classics available. He also printed grammar guides and dictionaries to assist scholars in their study of these materials.

Desiderius Erasmus, one of the most famous classical scholars of the sixteenth century, provides an exemplar of the relationship between the printed book and humanist scholarship. Erasmus's scholarly focus was the unification of classical scholarship and Christianity, and print technology provided a vehicle for this. In 1502, his collection of 4,000 proverbs from classical texts was written and printed in Aldus Manutius's shop, in which Erasmus had resided for several years. The Basel printer John Froben, who oversaw the printing of Erasmus's Latin and Greek editions of the New Testament, also played host to the great humanist while the work was being completed. Indeed, Erasmus made a habit of living and working in print shops throughout Europe. Printing shops often turned into intellectual dens as the conversation conducted in their inner confines produced writings, and the writings in turn were disseminated in print.

EXPANSION AND PRODUCTION

One of the qualities often associated with technology is speed. Innovations are, to a large extent, intended to expedite various functions. Just as trains made transportation more efficient, and text messaging today has quickened the pace of communication, the printing press allowed material to reach the hands of interested parties much faster than manuscript ever could. Whether it was the issuance of a papal bull (a mandate of the Pope) or the posting of a merchant's new stock, the press allowed information to be widely distributed in a matter of days. New works were sent across Europe and eagerly sought after, as friends obtained copies for friends. Suddenly, the networks of book exchanges burgeoned. By 1500, they were a regularly traded commodity among private readers and professional booksellers.

No printer exemplifies the growth of printing in this period better than Christophe Plantin (1520–1589), a Frenchman counted among the most famous and influential individuals in the history of book production. In 1555, this printer, publisher, bookbinder, and bookseller established a printing house in Antwerp, after spending seven years as a bookbinder and leather worker.

While Venice had enjoyed a position at the center of global trade in the fifteenth century, Antwerp and her sister cities in the Low Countries— today's Netherlands and Belgium—rose to prominence in the sixteenth century, supplanting the supremacy of Venice. The Low Countries proved to be fertile ground for the establishment of printing shops. In the first forty years of the century, 133 printers established shops in the Low Countries, half of these in Antwerp (Clair 1960, 11).

Competition between print shops was intense. Plantin wanted some assurance of success in his new venture, and so in 1563, he entered into a business contract with four of Antwerp's most successful merchants. Together, they established one of the first corporate printing houses, *De Gulden Passer* (The Golden Compasses). The merchants supplied capital and Plantin was at once master printer and manager, and for his services he received an annual salary. His job required familiarity with all phases of the printing operation, from typecasting to binding. The only aspect of the business from which Christophe was excused was accounting: for this the venture capitalists hired a bookkeeper.

This high-structured and well-supported business model afforded the Plantin shop freedom to undertake a wide variety of printing projects. Jobs from the Catholic Church, which needed books in large quantities and had a deep pocketbook to pay for them, kept the corporate coffers filled. The Golden Compasses's largest church project came in 1563. Church officials, meeting at the Council of Trent, decided to standardize the missals being used in every parish, from England to southern Italy. This would prove a monumental printing project, and Plantin, working through a patron, obtained a monopoly on the right to print the new liturgical works for all of the Low Countries.

Not satisfied with fortifying his dominant business position with this tremendous contract, Plantin sought a more typographically challenging project, one that would bring his printing house glory. Supported—at least initially—by Philip II, king of Spain, Plantin undertook the production of a multilingual version of the scriptures in Hebrew, Greek, Latin, Chaldaic, and Syriac: a polyglot Bible. The project required that Plantin secure a different font of type for each language and hire editors fluent in the languages involved. In an effort to keep his highly accomplished Hebrew editor on staff, Plantin arranged this editor's marriage to one of his daughters. As in the days of Fust and Schöffer, familial unions often cemented valuable business relationships.

The polyglot Bible was printed in 1569, but with little support from Philip II. The king had found his treasury depleted and, despite repeated promises, ultimately reneged on his commitment of financial support to Plantin. Despite this setback, the work was printed and—though quite expensive—made ready for sale.

Plantin's shop (the *Officina Plantiniana*) was proto-industrial; at its peak, it housed twenty-one presses, and produced more than 1,500 works over its life. Plantin's printer's device, a hand holding a geometer's compass, bore the famous motto *Labore et Constantia*, or Labor and Perseverance. The mark signaled quality throughout Europe.

Plantin's business records, preserved in his shop-turned-museum in Antwerp, show that in 1565, about one-half of Plantin's total investment went toward the raw materials of printing. Paper was the biggest expense, counting approximately 75 percent of the cost of making a book (only 20 percent went to labor) (Gaskell 1995, 177–179). Securing a source of high-quality paper at an affordable price was a constant struggle for printers in Europe. Demand constantly exceeded supply, and regional conflicts often threatened even that tenuous supply. Periodic embargoes could bring an entire print shop to a halt. Still, printing was an extremely profitable trade. The sale price of a book, according to Plantin's records, was two to three times the cost of production.

TRAVELS FROM HOME: BOOK FAIRS IN EUROPE

In the days before the printing press, manuscripts were traded locally and internationally through networks of clerics, scholars, scribes, merchants, and aristocrats. This exchange necessarily became more dynamic with the introduction of the printing press, as the sheer number of books in circulation increased exponentially. Emerging in the late fifteenth and early sixteenth centuries, the book fair drew on a long tradition of religious and commercial gatherings. With a host of publishers, authors, and booksellers gathered together, hundreds of books could be perused, purchased, and bartered with ease—eliminating many of the expenses normally involved in sales.

Since booksellers gravitated toward those places where people gathered, goods were traded, and business deals forged; one of the earliest book fairs took place in Lyon, in the south of present-day France. Long before books were the key commodity traded there, Lyon's fair featured a robust trade in spices and silk—goods making their way from east to west. But as printed books gained in popularity and major presses established themselves, the fair became a focal point for booksellers from all over the Continent. Italian books moved north to England and France through Lyon, in the same way that German books were taken from the fair back to Venice and Rome. In the mid-sixteenth century, Lyon's book fair was the place to go in Europe to find recent publications, the most current printing technology, and the most influential printing houses.

Not long after Lyon's fair was established, another emerged in Frankfurt, again as an outgrowth of a local fair that had existed long before printed books. In what might be considered a family reunion, publishers from all over the Continent—including Italy, Holland, France, Germany, and Switzerland—came together to sell and exchange their books in Frankfurt twice a year: once during Lent (before Easter) and again at Michaelmas (before Christmas). In 1569, fair records showed that there were eighty-seven booksellers on hand. Type-designers, typecasters, engravers, compositors, editors, and hopeful authors all attended the fair in hopes of selling their goods or services. All the apparatus needed to run a print shop was available at this two-week trade expo.

Printing houses busily prepared for this fair, ensuring that their most promising works were ready in time to be shipped. A young printing-house employee noted that "the Frankfurt Fair was imminent, and the printers were clamouring for the copytext I had promised them" (Jardine 1996, 226). Even if only a small print run was possible in time for the fair, it was better for a printer to showcase his offerings and sell out than fail to bring fresh material to such a robust marketplace. However, most printers were ready with fairly large print runs—up to 2,000 copies of a book—confident that they would either sell or be traded for books by other sellers.

Stock swapping at the fair was an efficient way to enrich a shop's offerings without losing cash, which was always in short supply. Through this system of trade, a work printed in Holland had a chance at reaching a much wider readership, and publishers—who would otherwise be limited to the small markets of their town—could sell their stock to numerous interested buyers. Christophe Plantin, who attended the fair every year until his health deteriorated (whereupon he sent a representative), even purchased storage for the books he had left over at the end of the fair. These would be taken out for the next fair, saving him the trouble of shipping the books back and forth between Frankfurt and Antwerp.

Within a few years, buyers at the Frankfurt Fair encountered such a variety of products and agents that a catalog of both books and booksellers had to be created. These catalogs provide today's historians with a wealth of information: What books were printed? What was their format? Folio? Quarto? Who were their authors? Between 1564 and 1600, the catalogs for the Frankfurt Fair listed over 20,000 titles (Febvre and Martin 1990, 231).

The Frankfurt Fair was a key stimulus to the expansion of the book market, but it declined in the seventeenth century due to religious conflict and warfare. Ironically, the very industry that had flourished in part due to a flood of religious books and pamphlets now suffered at the hands of church censors, who often preferred burning to reading.

DISCIPLINE: BANNED BOOKS

The body most often credited with programmatically banning books was the Inquisition, a council of church leaders that met regularly to discuss issues of faith and formal doctrine. They also opined on appropriate reading material for the laity.

The Inquisition was created in the thirteenth century by Pope Gregory IX as a scholarly body dedicated to inquiry into theological issues of the day. The Inquisition changed, however, in response to the turbulence of the Crusades and the presence of Muslims and Jews on the Iberian peninsula. In the wake of the violent expulsion of the "unfaithful," the Spanish Inquisition was formed in 1498. Its purpose was to unify and perhaps purify the Spanish faithful, and to rid Spain of any influences that ran counter to the church's teachings. The result was the imprisonment and execution of thousands who were accused of heresy.

The Inquisition's strict policies about printed books were an integral part of this effort to create a unified Catholic hegemony. Those books considered a threat to the Holy Roman Catholic Church were banned not just in Spain, but in the Low Countries as well. Present-day Belgium and Holland were still under the rule of Spain and therefore required to abide by the mandates of the Spanish Crown.

On May 8, 1529, Charles V—king of Spain and Holy Roman Emperor—issued a ban on all books by Martin Luther, ordering them burned. Printers found producing Luther's works—or the works of his sympathizers—could be tried for treason, and if found guilty, executed. Six months later, this policy was officially enunciated:

> it is universally forbidden to print, read, or to have supported the writings, books or doctrines of Martin Luther: together with many other heretics and their books and other things of this nature. (Clair 1960, 106n1)

Such a mandate was not unusual in the sixteenth century, as the church attempted to stem the tide of Reformation literature streaming off printing presses throughout Europe. Gutenberg's technology introduced the most challenging threat yet faced by the clerical establishment, and the number of books that the church felt were "dangerous" in the hands of the laity grew rapidly. One by one, they were added to the list of books pronounced illegal to print.

Naturally, the list of banned books was not static. The church made every effort to keep pace with the printers and pressmen, and regularly issued updates to their lists of banned books. And each updated list came with renewed threats against those who participated in trade of illicit material. The Spanish Crown issued a catalog of 295 prohibited books in 1546; in 1551, sixty-nine books were added, and by 1559, there were 650 books listed (Clair 1960, 106–107). Moreover, Spanish administrators required that these lists be posted in every bookshop, and their officers fanned out through the cities to ensure that booksellers were abiding by the rule. Shops without the list of banned books posted were subject to fines and, no doubt, a very thorough inspection of the premises.

For church officials in Rome, however, these actions on the part of the Spanish Crown proved to be a significant burden. Pope Paul III had organized the "Sacred Congregation of the Roman Inquisition" in 1542, but it took—at least initially—a more modest approach to religious reform than Spain had undertaken. From Rome's perspective, the Spanish Inquisition's efforts to root out heretical books had unwittingly created an administrative nightmare. It was impossible for church officials to consider every printed book to determine whether it violated the doctrine enough to warrant banning. Eventually, the requirements outlined by the Spanish Inquisition went beyond those that Roman officials had drawn up for themselves at the Council of Trent in 1546. To the pontifical leadership in Rome, it seemed the Spanish had stretched their authority too far, creating a censorship policy that was inconsistent and impossible to prosecute.

But the catalogs of banned books kept coming, updated frequently, as censors tried in vain to keep up with Europe's printing presses. In 1555, Pope Paul IV changed the tenor of the Roman Inquisition by opening a vigorous campaign to purge Italy of all unauthorized or heretical books. The Index of Forbidden Books was first published in 1559 and would be updated thereafter. (The issue published in 1948 lists 4,000 titles. The Index was finally discontinued in 1966.)

Some printers, such as Christophe Plantin, turned the situation to their advantage, procuring lucrative contracts with the church for the exclusive right to print their books. In the 1560s and 1570s, Plantin's presses issued numerous indices listing prohibited books, each one entitled *Index Librorum Prohibitorum*. Not only did Plantin win the contract, but in 1570, he was appointed "proto-typographer" (or printer-in-chief) by Philip II of Spain. In this newly created role, Plantin was charged with overseeing sixty-two printers in his assigned region in the Low Countries. He ensured that they were qualified printers with a solid understanding of all aspects of the business (from composition to binding). Plantin also did the equivalent of "background checks," making certain that no one who sought an official license to print had a history of publishing illicit material. Though much of the job was a formality, it reflects the degree to which printed books—and the printers who made them—threatened the church.

Plantin was able to thrive economically by playing pressman to the church. Most printers, however, did not enjoy Plantin's close relationship with the church authorities, and many of them turned to the covert production of banned titles for their economic survival. Banned books, then as now, enjoyed interest among readers who might not have paid them any attention otherwise. The very scarcity of these books often served to increase their desirability. Many were best-sellers. It only required some ingenuity and a few trusted pressmen to see them into print.

THE OFFSPRING MOVE OUT: BOOKS IN THE COLONIES

While books were thriving and evolving in the Old World, the sixteenth and seventeenth centuries saw the expansion of print technology around the globe. Covering the history of this diaspora would require volumes, but to understand the influence of European bookmakers, one need only look to the Western Hemisphere.

The British Colonies

The first printed works in North America arrived with the English colonists on the *Mayflower*. Initially, books were supplied by printers back home: well-established firms in Antwerp and London were more than willing to augment their workload—and income—to satisfy colonial readers. But ultimately, print culture—like other cultural artifacts—would be assimilated into colonial life, and books would take on the unique characteristics of their new homes.

The first books printed in the English colonies came from a press in Massachusetts, but perhaps unsurprisingly, all the hardware involved in the printing process was imported from Europe. In 1638, Mrs. Jose Glover, the widow of an America-bound printer who died en route, established a press that was affiliated with Harvard University. Run by Matthew Day, the Harvard press was fully operational by 1639. Day was responsible for printing a variety of single-page broadsheets and religious pamphlets, as well as the first colonial book: *The Bay Psalm Book*, printed in 1640, of which 1,700 copies were issued.

Upon Day's death, Samuel Green took over the Harvard press. In a move that reflects the undeveloped state of print culture in the colonies, Green had to advertise for an assistant back in England, since there was no qualified person to be found around Boston. He ended up with Marmaduke Johnson. Together, Green and Johnson issued the first complete Bible printed in the American colonies: the *Eliot Indian Bible* of 1663. Translated into Algonquian by the Puritan minister John Eliot, the Bible (whose transliterated title was *Mamvsse wunneetupanatamwe up-biblum God*) provided missionaries with a much-needed resource in their conversion efforts among indigenous peoples. This was the largest printing project in the colonies to date; nothing would come close to its size until midway through the eighteenth century. Because the financial resources of the missionaries were relatively minimal, the book was underwritten by England's "Corporation for Propagation of the Gospel in New England and Parts Adjacent in America," a religious organization chartered in 1649 for the purpose of converting indigenous Americans.

Book production relied on such English subsidies in the early years of the colonies, and given their small population and conservative political climate, support for new printing operations was not forthcoming. Following the establishment of Harvard's press, it was decades before another print shop was established in the colonies and fifty years before a paper mill was introduced. In 1674—over thirty years after Harvard's press—the very capable Bostonian, John Foster, set up another press. A teacher, mathematician, and engraver, Foster founded his press at the sign of the Dove and found success printing maps, broadsides, and books. Though he died at only thirty-three years of age, his achievements were recognized at his funeral in the following verse:

Adde to these things I have been hinting
His skill in that rare ART OF PRINTING
His accurate Geography
And Astronomick Poetry;
And you would say 'twere pitty He
Should dy without an Elegie. (Green 1893, 3)

Foster's Boston-based press was followed by another, belonging to William Bradford, which he established in Philadelphia in 1685. The decade-long gap between the establishment of these presses can be attributed to the relatively small and widely dispersed population of the colonies, which translated into lower demand for reading material. Colonial towns could seldom justify the expense of their own press. William Rittenhouse established the first paper mill in 1690 next to Bradford's print shop, but it would remain the only such papermaking site in the colonies for the next twenty years. Demand—even from newspapers—was not high enough to warrant additional mills.

Until independence, most colonists were content to read books shipped over from England. Even when local printing offices were established, they tended to focus on printing municipal works—flyers and broadsheets of a utilitarian or governmental nature—or newspapers, which became the bedrock of the printing industry in North America.

Also contributing to printing's slow start in the colonies was a strong resistance among local colonial officials to having books printed and circulated. Indeed, they made programmatic efforts to limit freedoms of printers. Having seen what resulted in England from years of uncensored book publication, English officials in the colonies regularly articulated their reticence about allowing the technology of the book to take hold in their lands. In 1671, Sir William Berkeley, the then governor of Virginia, thanked God that "there are no free schools nor printing, and I hope we shall not have [them] these hundred years; for learning has brought disobedience, and heresy, and sects into the world, and printing has divulged them, and libels against the best government. God keep us from both." Printers who ran afoul of the law faced serious penalties for violating Licensing Acts, which—until the end of the seventeenth century—regulated what could be printed. The more docile of the punishments included time in jail, while the more draconian involved cutting off the ears of the violating printer. Few books were worth such a price.

It was not until the eighteenth century that printing became firmly established in the colonies. When it was, the move was largely spurred by the newspaper industry, not the book market. "Printer-journalists" sprung up along the eastern seaboard and printing shops labored to keep up with the demand for current news. Presses that may have been established to meet newspaper demands (and reap the financial rewards of news printing), would eventually move into the book market.

Naturally, the events surrounding the American Revolution were informed by, and had an impact on, printers. Much of the printed material related to the revolution appeared in broadside or newspaper form, fueling the fire of colonial discontent and giving printers a central place in the national debate. Benjamin Franklin, who contributed immensely to the printing and publishing development of the colonies, published an article in the *Pennsylvania Gazette* on May 27, 1731, which defended printers who—through their craft—became embroiled in the partisan politics of independence:

> I request all who are angry with me on the Account of printing things they don't like, calmly to consider . . . [that] Printers are educated in the Belief, that when Men differ in Opinion, both Sides ought equally to have the Advantage of being heard by the Publick; and that when Truth and Error have fair Play, the former is always an overmatch for the latter . . . I consider the Variety of Humours among Men, and despair of pleasing every Body; yet I shall not therefore leave off Printing. I shall continue my Business. I shall not burn my Press and melt my Letters. ("Apology for Printers")

Ben Franklin's efforts in the history of American printing—especially newspaper, pamphlet, and book production—are notable both for his technical contributions and for his ability to create markets for printed material. Simply put, he was the most economically successful printer in the colonies and among the most important figures in the history of American print culture.

As a young man, Franklin had been introduced to the world of book production through his older brother John, a London-trained printer who took young Benjamin on as an apprentice. When his elder sibling encountered legal troubles, Franklin was assigned the responsibility of managing their newspaper, the *New England Courant*. On February 4, 1723, Ben Franklin's name appeared on a half-sheet issue of the paper, his first solo effort in printing. A trip to England in 1724 was intended to allow Franklin to purchase printing equipment not available in the colonies, but money problems led him to work as a journeyman for two of London's well-known printers, Samuel Palmer and, later, James Watt.

> At my first admission into [Watt's] printing-house I took to working at press, imagining I felt a want of the bodily exercise I had been us'd to in

America, where presswork is mix'd with composing . . . [but] Watts, after some weeks, desiring to have me in the composing-room, I left the pressmen. . . . My constant attendance (I never making a St. Monday) recommended me to the master; and my uncommon quickness at composing occasioned my being put upon all work of dispatch, which was generally better paid. So I went on now very agreeably.

In addition to learning the skills of a compositor and a pressman, Franklin gained valuable insight into the operation of a print shop. He returned to Philadelphia two years later and set up his own establishment. This he managed at every level, from selecting the jobs to setting the type to arranging distribution.

In 1730, Franklin became the official printer to the state of Pennsylvania, and the following year, he established the Library Company of Philadelphia, an organization that made books readily available to the public. Through his appreciation of the printing craft, and his political influence, Franklin helped establish printing houses throughout the colonies.

Though he was highly successful in running the *Pennsylvania Gazette*, Franklin remains best known for *Poor Richard's Almanack*, which—under Franklin's guidance and the pen name Richard Saunders—came out each December from 1733 through 1758. These almanacs were tailored to agrarian interests, offering farmers advice about planting, harvesting, and weather, as well as moral advice. In marketing his almanacs, Franklin made a foray into the realm of creative advertising. His "Preface to Courteous Readers"—ostensibly signed by the very Richard Saunders of the title—begins:

I might in this place attempt to gain thy Favor, by declaring that I write Almanacks with no other View than that of the public Good; but in this I should not be sincere; and Men are now a-days too wise to be deceived by Pretenses how specious so ever. The plain Truth of the Matter is, I am excessive poor, and my Wife, good Woman, is, I tell her, excessive proud; she cannot bear, she says, to sit spinning in her Shift of Tow, while I do nothing but gaze at the Stars; and has threatened more than once to burn all my Books . . . if I do not make some profitable Use of them for the good of my Family. The Printer has offered me some considerable share of the Profits, and I have thus begun to comply with my Dame's desire.

It is impossible to know whether or not the public bought into this fiction, but the fact remains that the book sold at a rapid clip. In Philadelphia, with a population around 15,000 people, 10,000 copies of *Poor Richard's Almanack* were sold (Wright 1986, 55). The only book with greater circulation at the time was the Bible.

As Franklin's business grew, he fostered a series of relationships with printers in other cities, many of whom were former employees. From South Carolina to New York, in cities like Newport, Boston, and Annapolis, Franklin enjoyed close working relationships with printers, allowing his works to be sold in their shops. By extending the reach of his press, he turned his newspaper and book-printing business into a resounding financial success. Between 1729 and 1766, Franklin—along with his partner David Hall—issued nearly 1,000 imprints—books, pamphlets, and broadsides included (Winterich 1974, chap. 4).

After 1776, the story of printing in the colonies would soon become the story of printing in an independent United States. The nineteenth century would see America emerge at the forefront of global book production, with its printers contributing to the rapid industrialization and mechanization of printing.

South America

Just as books were carried to the shores of North America by British and French colonists, so too were they brought into South America by Spanish and Portuguese explorers. With the influx of New World books, it should not be assumed that indigenous cultures lacked a book culture of their own. On the contrary, despite strong oral traditions, pre-Hispanic societies in the Americas used texts of all kinds.

The indigenous cultures of Mesoamerica, around present-day Mexico, recorded many aspects of life and culture in pictograph form. Images depicting rituals and historical events were recorded on textiles and pottery, much in the tradition of papyrus scrolls in Africa, or Sumerian clay tablets. Pre-Columbian works of the Maya and the Aztec consisted of painted images on a series of animal skins or a thin bark, known as amatl. These were nearly identical to the early European manuscripts, except that in many cases the indigenous works were not bound. Instead, the leaves were glued together and the entire work was folded accordion-style.

These painted works from Mesoamerica, containing both images and texts, are known as codices. A well-known example is the Codex of Coyotepec, an Aztecan work produced in the sixteenth century. The Codex, with its pages of animal skin and its pictorial record of events and rituals, reflects the state of indigenous book culture in Mexico before the introduction of European printing techniques.

Other indigenous books dealt with herbal remedies, tasks of daily life, and religious ceremonies. For the conquering Spanish, these works proved invaluable for understanding the New World culture and—in many cases—appropriating New World knowledge.

Page from the Codex of Coyotepec, an indigenous work that preceded the arrival of the printing press in the Americas. Courtesy of the Library of Congress.

When the Spanish did arrive, first in the West Indies and then on the mainland of the Americas, they brought with them both religious and secular works. Initially, the audience for these books was the conquistadors themselves, who embraced both the romantic tales of Spanish chivalry as well as the religious texts intended for use in ministering to native peoples. Benefiting from this robust market of conquerors and converts were European printers such as Christophe Plantin in Antwerp, whose contracts with the church to print missals and other religious material proved especially lucrative as Spanish colonial influence grew.

It was not long before presses themselves were established in the New World, largely in response to the growing demand for books. Unlike in Europe, where readers had developed a taste for a variety of printed books—from the highly spiritual to the highly entertaining—priests in Mexico and other colonies demanded little other than the word of God.

Juan de Zumárraga, bishop of Mexico, was responsible for establishing the region's first printing press and paper mill. In 1539, he sought permission from the Crown to build both, and his request was granted. Five years later, the *Dotrina breve . . . de las cosas que pertenecen a la fe catholica* (Brief doctrine . . . on things related to the Catholic faith) was printed. A copy of this rare work held in the British Museum is the oldest surviving printed work from Mexico. While Zumárraga's press focused on clerical books, subsequent presses—such as that of Juan Pablo—printed primers for native children. The nicer volumes printed in the colonies were bound in leather and tooled in gold for decoration, but more commonplace books were bound in vellum cases. The titles were often written by hand on the spine, and the sewing of the binding was of mediocre quality.

Over time, the output of colonial presses expanded. By the end of the sixteenth century, over 116 different books had been printed in Mexico City, and by the end of the seventeenth century, this number had increased to over 1,000 titles (Febvre and Martin 1990, 209). And other parts of Latin America shared this growth in book production. Antonio Ricardo, a printer from Italy, established a press in Lima in 1584, which catered to the needs of the Peruvian Jesuits and wealthy Spanish bureaucrats who had assumed administrative roles and settled in the region. With a population of more than 10,000 people, Lima afforded printers a readership eager for new books, so much so that Ricardo commenced printing before receiving the official sanction from Philip II, on August 7, 1584, that the Viceroyalty of Peru could legally operate its own press. Among the first books printed in Peru was a trilingual catechism (book about religious principles), printed in Spanish, Quechua, and Aymara.

Printing presses were subsequently established in other parts of South America, expanding slowly through colonial towns and dedicated to spreading the Christian doctrine. As independence movements formed, colonists in the Southern Hemisphere used the press in much the same way their northern neighbors had: printing pamphlets, broadsides, and books that reflected their sense of nationalism and hope for independence.

Upon emancipation from their imperial rulers, printing technology continued to develop in the postcolonial world, albeit more slowly than in North America. By the time the United States and Great Britain had moved into the era of steam-powered presses, many of the Latin American printing houses retained the handpress. Even so, the books produced recorded and reflected the values and interests of pre- and postcolonial America.

4

Adulthood: Early-Modern Books, 1600–1800

London, January 1640. It is 5:00 AM—well before anyone is awake—and the master of the local printing house has already risen from bed and made his way downstairs to his shop. Once his father-in-law's shop, he inherited it and the adjacent bookshop three years ago, along with its considerable debt. Now, it was his to run, with—occasionally—his wife handling some of the financial affairs of the shop.

On this chilly morning, the master sets to work on tasks that require his full attention: reviewing the ledgers, confirming the day's print jobs, calculating the shop's paper needs, and—with what time is left—giving a cursory glance to yesterday's production. By 7:00 AM the men would be arriving, some to run the shop's two presses, others to compose and ink type. Their loud conversations, their heaves as they pulled the press, the cries for more ink or paper, would soon fill the little shop with the commotion of production.

His resources were, of course, limited. In addition to his presses, he had managed to procure fourteen fonts of type, ornaments and initials for decoration, and a set of tools for his workers. But his skills as a printer were truly excellent, and his craftsmanship had earned him a strong reputation in town.

Books that emerged from the master's press would be sold in his shop, and if he has time before the day begins, he will check the stock there as well. His publishers would be unforgiving if they did not find their books clearly displayed. Most of what his shop printed was commissioned by publishers, a system that suited him just fine. His reputation for producing quality books—procuring good paper and having the best type in the city—earned him enough business to keep the shop going, if just barely.

On rare occasions, the master himself procured printing jobs. Acting as publisher, he contracted with the author for the manuscript, saw to its printing, and arranged for the book to be sold—both in his own shop and those in other cities. But even part-time publishing meant days of correspondence with both authors and booksellers, obtaining and editing the manuscripts, and then arranging the sale and distribution of the book. Publishing meant orchestrating a series of exchanges through a network of booksellers, and this master printer was content to limit his participation in such a complex mercantile system. Nor would he have wanted to be a printer alone. Shops that printed and left the sales to others struggled to stay afloat when the jobs dried up, as they invariably did.

A few minutes after 7:00 AM, the men begin to arrive, some slightly groggy from what must have been a long night. By the sixteenth century, many journeymen in the printing business had bonded together into "brotherhoods," as was increasingly common for skilled craftsmen at the time. Masters who ran printing houses were faced with a more organized labor force. In this year alone the brotherhoods of London, complaining of insufficient wages, had called for no fewer than three strikes, though only one of those came to fruition.

Though unified under one banner, journeymen printers had their own hierarchies: a head compositor, whose language skills placed him above others working in the shop; skilled workmen—other compositors or typesetters; and pressmen, whose qualifications amounted to little more than thick forearms and a penchant for manual labor. But despite the variations in skill, journeymen were united by their common apprenticeships and their collective status in the printing house. Each had been trained in every aspect of printing, from the setting of type to pulling the press, and each had spent time "abroad"—journeying to cities beyond their home to earn valuable experience in their chosen trade. When they settled—in their native cities or elsewhere—they contributed a valued skill-set and a remarkable work ethic.

The master could expect his journeymen to work a 12-hour day, though legal limits on the workday were constantly changing. Their wages, especially those of pressmen, were equivalent to earnings of an unskilled craftsman, a roofer, for example (Febvre and Martin 1990, 133). This despite their ability to turn out over 3,000 pages of printed text in a single day, each page requiring a hefty pull of the press. Organizing into guilds, however, gave the journeymen a much-needed lever to negotiate with the master printers who hired them. Insufficient pay or poor working conditions would quickly result in a walkout, a nasty predicament for a master in the middle of an important print job. There was always other work to be done, and the independent-minded journeymen felt no obligation to a particular shop, especially one in which they felt their services were not appreciated. The master's hands were often tied in such situations. He could appeal to the local council and hope for their mediation in a particularly difficult labor situation, but the results of such an appeal would rarely be a return to work. Arriving at the shop this morning, however, the journeymen seem ready to start work.

Despite the sunshine, near-freezing temperatures in the unheated ground floor presented a challenge to the typesetters. Their nimble fingers, reaching into the cases to retrieve thousands of sorts over the day, would be slowed by the chill. And though the pressmen's labors kept them relatively warm, the ink would be thickened by the cold air and the moistened paper rigid with hoarfrost. It would be important to hang the sheets high in the rafters—the "chapel" as the men called it—to dry, where they would receive the rising heat of the shop.

By 10:00 AM the journeymen had made noticeable progress on the day's jobs: an anonymously authored book about the East India trade and George Abbot's *The whole booke of Job paraphrased or, made easie for any to understand,* a book guaranteed to sell quickly. As was his custom, the master opted to print the works simultaneously to ensure that both of his presses would be in constant use, and his workers' hands constantly occupied. Unoccupied pressmen could be trouble; with the ability to pull one sheet every twenty seconds, they could quickly outpace the compositors and find themselves with free time, which was rarely used to the master's approval. Just last week the master had to intervene on several occasions when, unoccupied with work, the men gripped mugs of ale in lieu of press handles, pulling enough swigs of the ale to render them noisy and somewhat inefficient.

After a long morning of printing, work was suspended at noon and the journeymen went home for lunch. They were legally entitled to an hour's break—though most would extend this—and each man chose to take his break at home. The master, however, enjoyed no such luxury. He would remain in the shop, examining the galley proofs that would be printed in the afternoon. He shared this responsibility with a corrector—an educated man hired to read aloud the original manuscript so that the master could compare it with the printed proof. Along the way, he would fix typographical errors, insert spaces where the compositor neglected them, and check for the deterioration of particular letters. If a piece of type—the letter "b" for instance—was worn down, the image it produced in every copy would be compromised (increasingly so with each impression). It was critical to remove these poor pieces of type early and replace them with new sorts. The master's reputation hinged on printing a faithful and high-quality reproduction of the author's original manuscript—correcting proof was one of his most important duties.

With the lunch hour over, the master waited for his men to return. But the rest of the day would not go so smoothly. Though the compositors were back at work, setting type, the pressmen elected to stage a protest about wages—the second time this week—and they were refusing to come back. Faced with the possibility of not finishing the print job in time, the master had no alternative but to seek the help of lesser-qualified men, "hirelings" who could operate a press but lacked the experience of trained journeymen. They would have to do for the afternoon, and by bringing them on without hesitation the master hoped to send a message to his journeymen: they were not indispensable. These relatively unskilled hirelings, however, risked earning the ire of the journeymen by sliding so easily into their spots. They were the seventeenth-century version of strikebreakers and—disliked by both the journeymen they replaced and the masters who were forced into employing them—they were marginal figures in the world of print, unappreciated but somehow necessary.

By the day's end, the master's shop had printed just 1,800 sheets—hardly comparable to the normal 2,500 sheets a day. At 8:00 PM the workers went home, leaving the master and a young apprentice to stack the printed and dried pages, tidy up the compositor's station, and set up the supplies that would be necessary for tomorrow's jobs. With any luck, his journeymen would return, satisfied with the small increase in pay he had promised them.

The image of our master printer, and a comprehensive picture of printing in this period, comes into sharp focus through the work of Joseph Moxon. The quintessential English printer–publisher of the seventeenth century, Moxon was a craftsman—an instrument-maker as well as a printer—who proved an expert in all aspects of the trade. In 1678, he published the first of thirty-eight installments of his *Mechanick Exercises, or The doctrine of handy-works applied to the art of printing*. The second volume of this two-volume work was the first authoritative description of a printing operation, from the letter-cutters to the pressmen. In 450 dense pages, Moxon

explored the roles of all those involved in the production of a book. By selling his book in installments—or in serial—he ensured that lower-income
craftsmen could afford the work.

THE MIDWIVES TO PRODUCTION

The printed book is the immediate offspring of a press—a life that comes
into the world after a complex series of impressions and unions. This birth,
however, is only possible with the assistance of midwives: assistants who
guide it from its nascent stages into its matured form. As in the sixteenth
century, book production in the seventeenth century increased dramatically,
and the value of printed books dropped proportionally. What had been a
valued product of craftsmanship in the incunable era—its very ownership a
sign of status—became, under the influence of market forces, a standard
commodity, sold on every street corner from booksellers' stalls and stands.

With this increase in production, the roles of author, printer, publisher,
and bookseller became more clearly defined and, over time, increasingly specialized. New legislation clarified the rights and responsibilities of those
who produced books. And while the physical technology involved changed
little in the seventeenth and eighteenth centuries, the book itself sat at the
center of a revolution in information technology. Its importance was universally acknowledged: by merchant businessmen, by craftsmen, by esteemed
natural philosophers, and by members of Parliament who tried in vain to
control its contents. In less than 200 years the book had evolved from the
cradle to adulthood, a maturation that was evident in the increasingly complex web of people and places involved in its production and distribution.

Authors

Printed books are the product of a press, but long before the type is set, it is
the author's vision and voice that makes possible a book's existence. And in
the seventeenth century there was no shortage of willing authors. On topics from philosophy to theology to natural history, an increasing number of
writers sought to put their ideas into print.

But the author's existence cannot be taken for granted in discussions of
book history because, professionally speaking, there was no such career as
"author" until sometime back in the eighteenth century. In order for an individual to elect "author" as his vocation, there had to be some guarantee of
remuneration. The notion of profiting from writing, however, was frowned
upon in the seventeenth century, and the suggestion that an author could be

writing for pecuniary reward, rather than intrinsic devotion to the subject matter, called the author's credentials and motivations into question. Even if an author challenged this tradition and attempted to earn a living from his books, it is doubtful he would have earned enough from a publisher to survive.

This is one reason why the patronage system was so entrenched for authors. In return for dedicating a book to a wealthy aristocrat, the writer could hope for material compensation, as well as intellectual, political, and social support. In some cases, this was a stipend for lodgings and meals; to others, patrons offered a political appointment—easy enough to conjure up and hand out—which would supply the author with a level of comfort or security. In dedicating his 1659 book on the rings of Saturn to Prince Leopold dei Medici, the Dutch mathematician and astronomer Christian Huygens wrote:

> First, I have thought that your name, with such illustrious fame and abundant clarity, would reflect [well] on my work . . . in the second place, I am not ignorant of how much our discovery, consisting of a tentative explanation of the perplexing mysteries of Saturn, attains a certain importance if the honor of being approved by your exacting judgment were to fall upon it.

Prince Leopold, upon confirming that Huygens's theories were right, publicly endorsed the book and its ideas, lending Huygens considerable leverage in the intellectual battle he was waging with fellow astronomers, over Saturn's appearance.

Because of his wealth, Huygens needed no financial support for his work, but other authors offered such dedications for the express purpose of gaining financial backing. Unfortunately, hungry authors far outnumbered wealthy patrons, and few actually made a decent living this way, however flattering the dedicatory poems they composed. By the eighteenth century, this system was disappearing and authors began to be recompensed by publishers for their work. The great English writer of the century, Samuel Johnson, claimed that "We have done with patronage." With that assertion, the career of "author" was well on its way to being codified.

Yet, even as the era of commercial authorship eclipsed the era of patronage, authors remained bound in spirit to the ideal of writing for reasons other than financial gain. An inkling of the author's reluctance to publish for either money or fame can be seen in the "Prefaces to the Reader" in their books. Seventeenth-century prefaces were replete with excuses and caveats by the author: assertions that he did not really want to publish, accompanied by explanations as to why he or she had ultimately decided to do so. Many rationales were expressed: "My friends urged me to publish," "I felt the obligation to share the knowledge," or "A sinister opponent is threatening my reputation." But to admit to authorship for profit was akin to intellectual prostitution.

In the preface to his book *The Sceptical Chymist*, Robert Boyle goes to great length to explain that he wrote the work at the request of an "ingenious Gentleman," not for fame or financial gain. Moreover, he explains that it was "in complyance with [friends'] desires, that not only it should be publish'd, but that it should be publish'd as soon as conveniently might be." Left to his own devices, Boyle implies, he would not have sought publication, but at the behest of those close to him, he obliged.

Compounding this reluctance on the authors' part was the fact that they had no legal rights over their own intellectual property. The term did not even exist. In the seventeenth century, when an author deposited his manuscript at the printing shop or with a publisher, it was no longer under his control. He might receive recompense for it, but beyond whatever immediate payment he might get, he was at the mercy of the publisher and printer, who controlled the copy. On May 29, 1669, Christian Huygens wrote to a colleague in London, "If my consent were required to print my instructions for clocks I would gladly give it. But as it is already public property because of the edition I had printed in Dutch, I no longer have any rights in it."

This lament was echoed for more than 300 years by authors whose ownership of their manuscript ended at the print-shop porch. Once deposited with a master printer—or handed over to a publisher—it was the publisher who would benefit from the profits. Other printers who obtained a copy—legally or not—could also print the book for a profit, but all of this happened outside of the author's control. It was not until 1710 that legislation was passed in England granting authors control over their manuscripts. The copy that they deposited with printers became, in the eyes of English law, the author's property, and would remain so for a fixed period of time. (This will be discussed at length in a later section.) The rest of Europe lagged behind England on this matter, but by the end of the century, authorial rights were recognized in nearly every printing house and authors themselves found it much easier to make a living.

Editors

"How often we recall, with regret, that Napoleon once shot at a magazine editor and missed him and killed a publisher. But we remember with charity, that his intentions were good." Such was the recollection of Mark Twain, one of America's greatest authors and most fervent critics of editors. "I hate them," he wrote, "for they make me abandon a lot of perfectly good English words."

In today's book market the publication of an unedited book is rare. Major publishing houses staff editors for every genre, and even the most established authors benefit from their skills. But the editor's role in producing a book has not always existed. Until the seventeenth century, a manuscript would only be checked against the printed text by a corrector, and his concern was typographical errors, not the accuracy of the facts or the integrity of the claims, or the clarity of the writing. This was problematic, since errors could be introduced not only in setting the type, but in reading the copy, which would be in the author's hand—often illegible, as many historians can attest. In 1636, the famous mathematician and philosopher René Descartes wrote to a colleague:

> If you think that my manuscripts could be printed in Paris . . . and if you would be willing to take charge of them as you once kindly offered to do, I could send them to you immediately. . . . However, there is this difficulty: my manuscript is no better written than this letter; the spelling and punctuation are equally careless and the diagrams are drawn by me, that is to say, very badly. So if you cannot make out from the text how to explain them to the engraver, it would be impossible for him to understand them.

Descartes was not alone in soliciting the help of a friend to review his work and facilitate its publication. Many scholars found the prospect of publishing daunting enough that their manuscripts would never have become published books without the aid of a colleague or friend who, in modern terms, was acting as an editor. Though there was no such formal position, it is clear that by 1600 the category was evolving, however informally. Throughout the seventeenth century, examples abounded of scholars enlisting the expertise of colleagues or assistants as they shepherded their works to the press.

George Ent, a London physician and friend of the famous anatomist William Harvey, provides a good example of the emerging editorial role. Harvey is best known for his theory of circulation of the blood, on which he published a work in 1628. The publishing process proved difficult, however, and Harvey was uninterested in producing another book on his subsequent research. It was Dr. Ent who stepped in and encouraged him, promising to see the manuscript through to publication if Harvey would just write it. When Harvey's book, *Exercises on the Generation of Animals* was published in 1651, it opened with a dedicatory letter from George Ent, who described himself as a "midwife" who brought the book to birth, and that "he took particular care to oversee the printing, since he knew how much difficulty the compositor would have from the obscurity of Harvey's handwriting" (Keynes 1966, 332).

Ent's diligence in seeing Harvey's book produced testifies to the existence of a proto-editorial role in this period. Just over thirty years later, the great natural philosopher Isaac Newton would likewise benefit from the support and assistance of an editor—his colleague Edmond Halley, after whom the comet is named. In a story that echoes Harvey's, Halley approached Newton in 1684 and urged him to publish Newton's findings on universal gravitation. Newton, who had been subjected to the frustrations of publishing in the past, was reticent. But at Halley's insistence he agreed to have a book printed. The result was the famous 1687 *Mathematical Principles of Natural Philosophy*, or the *Principia*, after its Latin title. In his preface to the reader, Newton wrote:

> In the publication of this work, Edmond Halley, a man of greatest intelligence and of universal learning, was of tremendous assistance; not only did he correct the typographical errors and see to the making of the woodcuts, but it was he who started me off on the road to this publication . . . he never stopped asking me to communicate it to the Royal Society, whose subsequent encouragement and kind patronage made me begin to think about publishing it.

Any exploration of midwives to the seventeenth-century books cannot ignore the presence of men like Ent and Halley.

Publishers, Printers, and Booksellers

As the eighteenth century ushered in a new era of rights and recognition for authors, it marked an equally critical period of competition among publishers. Legally vested with ownership of an author's work, publishers had traditionally dominated the world of books. They arranged for an author's work to be printed, controlled the number of copies and editions run by the printer, and contracted the book's sale in various international shops. Major publishing houses, such as the Plantins in Antwerp and the Elzeviers in Amsterdam, reflected the size and dominance a successful publisher could achieve.

But increasing authorial rights, the emergence of private presses, and the operation of government presses all put a dent in the publisher's role.

Some authors opted out of the system entirely by printing their own books, preferring to incur the labor and costs themselves rather than deal with publisher's terms and the compositor's inevitable typographical errors. Major universities like Oxford and Cambridge started their own presses, thereby undercutting the market for textbooks that publishers had historically relied on for steady income. And to make matters worse, printers began to engineer new schemes for producing books that circumvented publishers entirely. One example is the sale of books by subscription. This clever technique was initiated in the seventeenth century and became widely popular in the eighteenth. It allowed the author to work directly with the printer, largely eliminating the publisher as middleman.

A book sold on subscription was advertised in bookshops and on flyers (or broadsides) posted throughout the city. Interested readers could sign up to pay a percentage of the book's cost in advance. This gave the printer ready cash with which to buy materials to print the work. In the traditional model, the printer and publisher would recoup their investment only after the book began to sell, a dynamic system that often required them to take out loans in order to start a new job. Subscriptions solved this dilemma. In return for their deposit on the book, subscribers' names were printed on a sheet inside the book and they were guaranteed a reduced price on it, once issued from the press. After subscriber orders were filled, the remaining copies could be sold for a higher price in bookshops. The author benefited, the printer benefited, and the subscribers benefited. Only publishers found the system wanting. Occasionally, printers and authors would arrange a book's production without a publisher involved at all, the author often moving into the printer's house to oversee the composition and printing.

In response to these changes in book production, publishing houses in the seventeenth century began to form the equivalent of joint-stock companies, called "congers," wherein publishers shared the investment in a particular work. Such partnerships meant more money could be invested up front, and there was a reduced risk of economic damage if the book failed to sell, since the loss would be distributed among investors. The conger, however, was only a stopgap measure. Authors and booksellers continued to challenge the hegemony of publishing houses, and all three maneuvered to better their position in the growing book business.

Whatever the level of their competition, publishers and booksellers had to work with each other on a regular basis, and both had an interest in how books were marketed and sold. Walking into a shop where one of his works was for sale, a publisher would expect to see the title of the book advertised—most likely on a flyer posted on the wall. Booksellers might even receive a small bonus from publishers if they displayed the title page of a book on the window, encouraging passersby to stop in and browse. But each bookshop played host to books from a number of publishers and presses, all of whom competed for display space. Ultimately, however, the bookseller had the final say. And if he had commissioned a work himself—acting as a publisher in his own right—it was only right that the book would be placed up front and center in the shop.

Throughout the rest of the shop, books would be piled on the rafters, most of them unbound, waiting to be sold. Those books that were sold with bindings tended to be more popular works, guaranteed to sell. Booksellers could hardly afford to bind a book, only to have it languish on the shelf.

For the majority of books, it was up to the purchaser to arrange for them to be bound. In some shops, they could order this directly from the seller, but a referral to a nearby bindery was not uncommon. There, a skilled leatherworker would bind the book according to the customer's preferences and budget. Binding techniques had evolved very little from those of the sixteenth century. The boards—or covers—were made of leaves of paper glued together to a certain thickness, and the spine was usually rounded and covered with paper. Endpapers, which cover up the stitching of the binding at the front and back of a book, were often decorated in the seventeenth century, enhancing the appearance of the work when opened.

If the volume was particularly prized by the consumer, a gold-tooled, sheepskin binding might be appropriate, though goat- and calfskin were readily available. The most magnificent bindings of the seventeenth and eighteenth centuries, however, were truly works of art. Adopting the ornate rococo style of the period, books would be bound in dyed leather, with lacework on the covers, and decorated spines. Such elaborate bindings, however, were the exception and not the rule. More commonly, a book would be bound in a "trade" binding. A standard calf- or sheepskin cover would be used, with little or no ornamentation. These bindings were essentially to protect the pages, adding little to the aesthetic value of the book.

Book prices were calculated by the sheet, and by the seventeenth century, these prices had dropped to such an extent that the "middling" classes—what we consider the middle class—could purchase a book on their relatively small wages. Each of Moxon's thirty-eight installments cost only six pennies: twelve pennies made one shilling, and the average artisan earned nineteen shillings per week. Thus, Moxon's installments cost the buyer less than 2 percent of his weekly income, a reasonable amount as far as artisans were concerned, and testimony to how affordable books had become.

Despite the financial safety net of the congers, publishers—and in turn printers—suffered in the supply-heavy market. Prices were low, profit margins meager, and competition was stiff. Though they were inextricably bound together by the larger world of print culture, by the eighteenth century, authors, printers, and publishers had organized themselves to better withstand the fluctuations in the market.

Case Study: The Elzeviers

This chapter's opening characterization of a master printer's daily life generalizes the experiences of printers in England, France, Italy, and the Low Countries in the seventeenth and eighteenth centuries. But one place in particular—the Low Countries—stands out in this period for the freedom its printers enjoyed and the profits they accrued. The Elzevier family—who immersed themselves in publishing, printing, and bookselling—sat at the center of the Dutch publishing world in the seventeenth century, a position from which they influenced the theological, classical, academic, and popular book market for 132 years.

Louis Elzevier (1546–1617) settled in Holland in 1580 after studying bookbinding and printing with Christophe Plantin in Antwerp. With start-up funds from Plantin himself, Elzevier opened a shop in Leiden, the famous university town, and began printing books for students. Undergraduates provided a captive market, eager for their own affordable copies of the classics. With their patronage, business grew rapidly and the Elzevier press expanded to The Hague, Utrecht, and—in 1638—to Amsterdam. These branches were run by the sons and grandsons of Louis: Joost, Abraham, Bonaventure, and Daniel. But it was under Louis's grandson Louis III that the Amsterdam operation made the Elzevier name famous across Europe.

In opening a printing house in Amsterdam, Louis III consciously placed print technology in one of Europe's commercial hubs. The Dutch East India Company had been founded in 1602, expanding the Low Countries' trade opportunities. The Amsterdam Exchange Bank—a major financier for merchants—was established in 1609. The Dutch dominated global trade, and Amsterdam, well situated at the center of the action, provided booksellers with abundant capital, eager investors, a sizeable reading public, and transportation readily at hand to carry books abroad. Melchoir Fokken's work *A Description of the widely renowned merchant city of Amsterdam*, first published in 1662, touted the city's international flavor and commercial productivity: "The Great and Almighty Lord has raised this city above all others . . . yea he has even taken from them the shipping of the east and

west . . . and has spilled their treasure into our bosom." Fokken's senti-
ments were echoed lyrically by the great Dutch poet of the day, Constan-
tijn Huygens, father of the previously mentioned astronomer. In praise of
Dutch riches, he penned the following verse in 1672:

> What is there that's not found here
> Of corn; French or Spanish wine
> Any Indies goods that are sought
> In Amsterdam may all be bought
> Here's no famine . . . the land is fat.

In addition to its thriving commercial activity, the Low Countries'
dearth of censorship laws proved attractive to authors, printers, publishers,
and booksellers alike. Having liberated themselves from Spanish rule in the
late sixteenth century, the Dutch were politically and religiously free, preferring Calvinism to Spain's Catholicism. This meant that publishers in the
Low Countries were not bound by the censorship of the Inquisition.
Works of all religious and political persuasions, books that would likely be
banned and confiscated in more religiously stringent cities, were welcomed
by Dutch publishers. By the end of the seventeenth century, Amsterdam
alone was host to over 270 printing houses that issued, among many others,
works of Thomas Hobbes, Galileo Galilei, and René Descartes: men whose
political, scientific, and philosophical leanings were scarcely welcome in
their homelands.

The Elzeviers's Amsterdam firm benefited from these tolerant policies.
Their business was located in a bustling part of the city, and its efficient ad-
ministration made it a profitable concern. In 1655, Louis III was joined by
his cousin Daniel in running the firm, and within the decade Daniel was in
full control of the printing house. Under his guidance, the Amsterdam shop
expanded its international network of booksellers by distributing its books
and book catalogs widely, and cultivating new clients at major book fairs.
Among their offerings, books on religion and politics ranked first, followed
by books on law, then the classics (such as Virgil, Seneca, and Cicero), and
finally, an assortment of French plays—pure entertainment. Their versions
of the classics were known for being well-edited, quality books—a trait not
often found in a book market that favored quantity over quality.

But the Elzeviers managed to obtain both, producing large print runs
of 2,500 to 3,000 books, which still upheld the high standards of the firm's
founders. In part, they were successful in these dual aims because they
printed small-sized editions: duodecimos (12×6 cm) that sold at an affordable price. Forty-two percent of the Elzevier books were this size, leading

many in the seventeenth century to use the term *Elzevier* synonymously with "small edition." But despite the size, these editions were first-rate—quality type, paper, and bindings—making them as attractive to consumers and collectors as their larger brethren.

The peak of Elzevier production began in the 1620s and ended in 1680, when Daniel died and the Amsterdam firm declined. The family also suffered financially from the impact of piracy, as other presses sought to emulate their small format and people bought up cheaper impressions of their works. Nevertheless, the Elzevier publishing firm stands out for its combination of business savvy and book quality. Set in the context of the Dutch Golden Age—a period of spirited trade and economic prosperity—the Elzeviers provide a good example of how large-scale publishers managed the manufacture of books in an ever-growing market.

PROTECTING YOUR KIN: COPYRIGHT AND PIRACY

In his famous dictionary, published in 1755, Samuel Johnson defined a pirate as "Any robber. Particularly a bookseller who seizes the copies of other men." While the modern notion of a pirate may involve an eye patch and ships full of treasure, to men of the seventeenth- and eighteenth-century publishing world, the term principally applied to those who stole the "copy" from an author or publisher. The term copy initially referred to the original manuscript produced by the author, but use of the term evolved, so that copy referred literally to "rights over a given copy" and thus, copyright.

The increasing number of books being printed led to a corollary increase in piracy, or theft of books from the original copyholders. Until the eighteenth century, piracy in its various forms was rampant. In some cases, a pressman might earn extra income by surreptitiously delivering galley proofs or manuscript pages to another press. That press would then secretly set the type on their own copy, hoping to produce a complete printed edition of the work before the shop that had been legitimately given the job. If they could do so, they would technically—in the eyes of the English law—be the rightful "owners" of that book.

Piracy also came from the printing of "supernumerary" copies, or extra copies in addition to those that the publisher had ordered. If 500 copies of a book were supposed to be printed, a master might discreetly have an additional fifty copies made, selling them for a profit on the side. There would be no shortage of bookstores interested in such copies, for they too would benefit from the lower cost. In the early days of printing, there was a tacit agreement between masters and journeymen that this practice of producing supernumerary copies was acceptable, but as the printing business organized, masters found it far more beneficial to simply pay the men the sum they would make on their additional copies, and clamp down on the supernumerary practice. Their efforts, however, were only marginally successful.

Other forms of piracy included selling an abridged version of a book— a crude summary that simply watered down what an author had written, without substantively changing any part of the text. Not only could these be produced quickly, but there was a ready audience interested in reading a condensed version of longer works. Translations also constituted a form of piracy, since the switch from Latin to French, for example, qualified the book as entirely original, according to the laws (Johns 1998, 489–490). Thus, a printer would hire someone to translate a Latin book into English, again appealing to a market of readers who were not trained in the ancient language but who still sought the stories or information contained in Latin books.

The net result of piracy was not just lower profits for printers and publishers, but a threat to the reputation of authors as well. It was not uncommon for pirated works to be of poor quality, riddled with typographical errors, mistranslations, and crude summarizations. Profit-oriented pirate printers cared little about quality, but authors were extremely concerned that the "knock-offs" would be attributed to them, damaging their character. In 1623, when Shakespeare's "First Folio" was published posthumously by his fellow actors John Heminge and Henry Condell, they commented on pirated copies in their preface. Their efforts, they claimed, would bring to the public Shakespeare's plays.

> As where (before) you were abus'd with diverse stolne, and surreptitious copies, maimed, and deformed by the frauds and stealthes of injurious imposters, that expos'd them: even those, are now offer'd to your view cur'd and perfect of their limbes . . .

Ultimately, piracy issues had to be dealt with through legal channels, and in this, the English led the way. Early in the fifteenth century, those associated with the production of books organized into a guild. Members of this guild became known as "stationers." Initially, their job was manageable, since manuscript books were produced at a relatively slow rate. But with the introduction of print technology, the demands on stationers grew and their ability to monitor and track the production of books was challenged.

In response to the increasing need for regulation, the London Stationers' Company was formed in 1557. This guild-like organization was backed by royal charter, and its wardens were charged with monitoring what was printed and seeking out illegal copies of books. Carpenters could not build a press without the Stationers' knowledge, and publishers could not legally have books printed outside of their purview. Though not every printed book in London from 1557 made it into the register—books issued from the Royal Press, for example, were exempt—the majority were registered. These records, which are kept in a similar form even today, provide historians with a rare and rich insight into the history of publishing practices of London. But in spite of the advantages of the company's register, problems with piracy persisted, and the issue of copy ownership continued to pose a problem—especially for authors who felt they were taken advantage of by publishers. Further legislation was needed.

Prior to the seventeenth century, legal mandates that dealt with books were almost universally of a censoring nature. A series of censorship laws enacted in the sixteenth and seventeenth centuries in England limited the freedom of publishers, printers, and authors to produce books. A legal body known as the Star Chamber issued decrees in 1586 and 1637 that imposed harsh penalties for the publication of illicit material. Similar action was taken by Parliament, which passed ordinances in 1643, 1647, and 1649 against the publishing of banned books. The Stationers' Company was assigned the task of pursuing those printers known to be producing banned works, and to see that such presses were physically dismantled.

During this period of stringent legislation, not only were printing shops destroyed, but booksellers caught peddling illegal texts were publicly whipped, and printing, in general, was limited to those specific masters who had received a special dispensation from the government. It was not a hospitable period for publishing "unwelcome" books. Toward the end of the seventeenth century, however, the censorship laws had an unanticipated effect: they indirectly protected the author's claim of ownership over his work. This ownership, in turn, meant that publishers could offer authors an advance in exchange for rights to a copy, and secure future revenues for themselves through publication of the copy.

The initial formalization of authorial rights came in 1662, with the Licensing Act, also known as the Press Act. This was called for by the English king Charles II, for "the better discovering of printing in corners without license" (Johns 1998, 131). The English had just emerged from civil war, and the new king (whose father had been executed in the war) was eager to suppress any seditious books and pamphlets.

With Parliament's passage of the Press Act, all booksellers had to be licensed, all printed books had to be registered with the Stationers' Company, and a copy of each book had to be placed on file. The Press Act reinforced the practice already in place, dating from the 1557 incorporation of the Stationers' Company. And while the intent of the act was to control printed products coming to market, the result was that ownership of a given copy was clearly identified. Piracy became much more difficult.

This licensing system—and the resulting protection of copyright—ended with the expiration of the Press Act in 1695. The Stationers' Company pleaded with Parliament to renew the act, but it would be over a decade before the problem was addressed. The solution finally came in the form of the Copyright Act of 1710, titled the "Act for the Encouragement of Learning by Vesting the Copies of Printed Books in the Authors, or Purchasers, of Such Copies during the Times therein Mentioned." The act—which effectively created the notion of authorial copyright—warrants repeating in full:

> Whereas Printers, Booksellers, and other Persons, have of late frequently taken the Liberty of Printing, Reprinting, and Publishing, or causing to be Printed, Reprinted, and Published Books, and other Writings, without the Consent of the Authors or Proprietors of such Books and Writings, to their very great Detriment, and too often to the Ruin of them and their Families: For Preventing therefore such Practices for the future, and for the Encouragement of Learned Men to Compose and Write useful Books; May it please Your Majesty, that it may be Enacted . . . That from and after the Tenth Day of *April,* One thousand seven hundred and ten, the Author of any Book or Books already Printed, who hath not Transferred to any other the Copy or Copies of such Book or Books, Share or Shares thereof, or the Bookseller or Booksellers, Printer or Printers, or other Person or Persons, who hath or have Purchased or Acquired the Copy or Copies of any Book or Books, in order to Print or Reprint the same, shall have the sole Right and Liberty of Printing such Book and Books for the Term of One and twenty Years, to Commence from the said Tenth Day of *April,* and no longer; and that the Author of any Book or Books already Composed and not Printed and Published, or that shall hereafter be Composed, and his Assignee, or Assigns, shall have the sole Liberty of Printing and Reprinting such Book and Books for the Term of fourteen [years].

What happened to copyright after the designated fourteen-year period was not made clear. This and other legal questions arose following the passage of this act, but it nevertheless had a transformative effect on the production of books. Whereas publishers had been vested with ownership of a copy before, now it was the author who held the property rights, and it was his or her obligation to ensure these rights by registering their works at the Stationers' office.

With this acknowledgment of intellectual property ownership, the author's role evolved dramatically and—if his work was at all popular—his pocketbook swelled. The author also had the option to sell his copyright to a publisher, who—if interested in the work of a popular author—offered good money to buy the rights to the work.

A concomitant effect of the Copyright Act was that piracy, in the town where the work was printed, nearly ceased. Either the author or the publisher legally owned the copy and had it registered with the Stationers' Company. Any illegal reproductions from other local presses were grounds for lawsuits against the printer who issued them. An entire underground market for early manuscript copies was thereby eliminated. Piracy abroad, however, remained a problem. Stolen copies were regularly printed internationally as printers and publishers sold the book (or galley proofs) to pirates in other cities.

BOOK INNOVATIONS: AUTHORIAL EFFORTS AND ENLIGHTENMENT DEVELOPMENTS

Printing and book technology were a central part of intellectual culture by the seventeenth century. Authors were plentiful and their products swamped the markets and depressed prices. In response to this stagnant climate, authors adopted various strategies to tilt the odds of financial success in their favor. Some pursued higher profits by circumventing the traditional publication channels. One such tactic was subscription sales, described above, which potentially cut out the publishers and brought the author and printer up-front payments. This method was increasingly employed in the eighteenth century. Other authors attempted to write for a broader audience, tailoring their work to a general readership and printing numerous, cheap copies of the book. Still others moved into the high-end book market. They learned the intricacies of bookmaking, from the manufacture of fine paper to the creation of a quality impression, with the hope that they could raise the level of craftsmanship in their works. The result would be a book that stood out in the bibliographic landscape.

Seventeenth-century scientists—men who explored what we now consider physics and mathematics—were among the authors who became actively involved in the printing craft. Some of the most famous works of natural history, mathematics, astronomy, and anatomy appeared in the seventeenth and eighteenth centuries, their authors well aware of the rapidly expanding audience for scientific books. Occasionally, their scientific interest was piqued by technical problems posed by the printing process, leading to the interesting juxtaposition of men of science improving the very means by which they were disseminating their discoveries.

One such scientist was Robert Hooke, Curator of Experiments from 1662 to 1703 for Britain's first scientific society, the Royal Society of London. Hooke wrote a letter to the well-known London publisher Moses Pitt in March 1679 about his "new contrivance for printing books," which involved tin plates and a rolling press (Inwood 2004, 266). Though his idea did not come to fruition, his instincts about the trajectory of printing technology were correct: in the late eighteenth century, the flat presses would be replaced with presses where paper passed through rollers to receive an impression. Hooke was an ardent tinkerer whose interest in machinery was equaled only by his interest in buying books, and he spoke to colleagues about printing techniques on several occasions. Though not a printer by trade, his interest nevertheless testifies to the desire some authors and bibliophiles felt to become more involved in the development of book technology.

Another scientist and mathematician who took an interest in printing technology was Christian Huygens, the Dutch polymath mentioned earlier. He is famous for—among other things—his discovery of Saturn's rings, the invention of a pendulum clock, and the development of wave theory of light. Huygens published numerous works in his lifetime and worked with some of the Low Countries' most notable publishers, including the Elzeviers. In the same way that he cultivated a technical knowledge of the construction of clocks and the building of telescopes, his work as an author acquainted him with the activities of a print shop. On May 19, 1669, he wrote to Henry Oldenburg, secretary for London's Royal Society:

> To give you new invention for new invention, I send you a sample of my new printing process in the leaf you see here. It is intended for printing writing and also for geometrical figures. It is cheap, and can quickly both engrave plates and print. Your Fellows will not find much difficulty in guessing how it is done; otherwise I shall provide an explanation if they wish.

With his new method, Huygens had printed a quotation from Virgil, but instead of presenting the quotation in type, he had printed material from his own handwriting. He invited his London friends to deduce the method just by looking at the printed sheet.

Several weeks later Oldenburg responded that several members (Fellows) of the Royal Society claimed to have developed a similar printing method, and that upon describing it they would send it to Huygens to compare the processes. According to Oldenburg, the physician William Petty had developed a printing method that allowed for as many copies as necessary to be printed while the book was on sale:

> and after an edition has been sold out it is possible to print a second, a third, and so on to any desired number . . . I do not know whether your method will print as many copies as one wishes, whether one can print with it matter that is printed already, and whether ordinary printer's ink is used. You will, if you please, inform us on these points. (Oldenburg to Huygens, May 31, 1669)

Huygens agreed that Petty's method sounded similar to his own, and in his reply he sent Oldenburg some new geometrical figures that he had printed with his method, though he still withheld the details of his process. This printed sheet was, like the Virgil quotation, in Huygens's hand rather than set in type, but nevertheless able to be reproduced as often as necessary.

On July 5, Oldenburg sent Huygens the Society's best guess for his printing method:

> I have shown our Fellows the geometrical figure which you have had printed by your new method. They ordered me to return you thanks, and Mr. Wren conjectures that you use the following method: Taking a brass plate as thin as paper you cover it with a varnish suitable for engraving and have the design drawn on that (taking care not to close up the letters) with such strong nitric acid as quite to pierce the brass. When this is done you turn the plate, putting it on another which is thicker and entirely coated with printer's ink; and then you pass it through a rolling press in the usual way. You will please tell us if Mr. Wren has described this correctly or not. Sir William Petty's method is different; but as he is not in England I have not permission to reveal it at present.

As it happened, several of the Royal Society men had guessed Huygens's technique correctly, except that instead of brass, the plates were copper, and instead of varnish, Huygens coated the plate with wax. Otherwise, the method was properly estimated.

The exchange between these gentlemen (not craftsmen) testifies to their deep understanding of the printing processes. The world of the printer's shop was not foreign to them, and their familiarity allowed them to make critical decisions about their own books as they went to press.

In the following century, this interest in printing among scholars and writers continued. In the literary arena, William Blake (1757–1827) stands out as an author who threw himself wholly into the production of unique and high-quality books, changing the nature of illustration along the way. Trained as an engraver, Blake cultivated a variety of creative interests: drawing, painting, sculpting, and composing poetry. In 1788, his artistic efforts coalesced in a new method of engraving, called relief etching. Using the traditional method of intaglio engraving, an artist would transfer an image from a page to the metal plate by tracing it—typically through wax. Blake's new method, however, cut out the tracing step so that the image was "painted" directly onto the copperplate with an acid-resistant varnish. When the drawing was completed, the plate was washed in an acid bath, which ate away the uncoated metal, leaving the acid-resistant image standing out of the plate in relief. This image—which, like old wood engravings, was in reverse—could then be inked and printed.

Blake employed his method of relief etching in his beautiful, illuminated books of poetry, such as *Songs of Innocence* and *The Book of Thel*, both

Title page of *Songs of Innocence*, published in 1789 by William Blake. Blake illustrated and published his own works with great artistry. Courtesy of the Library of Congress.

published in 1789. "If a method of Printing which combines the Painter and the Poet is a phenomenon worthy of public attention, provided that it exceeds in elegance all former methods, the Author is sure of his reward," he wrote. In his illuminated books, Blake combined a poem and an image on a single plate, so that each page was the product of a single impression. And, to fulfill the promise of illumination, each image was hand-colored by Blake and his wife (who helped him in all aspects of the printing), using watercolors they made themselves. The result was a book stunning in its appearance and revolutionary in its technique. Short of producing the paper, Blake created the entire book.

With copyright laws increasingly codified across Europe, and publishers eager to usher promising works to the press, the eighteenth century was an exciting time to be an author. But it was more than legal protection and potential profit that made this a fertile period in which to write. There was a cultural and intellectual movement afoot in Europe that revolutionized the way learned men thought about their God, their government, and their place in the world. We know this period as the Enlightenment, the "Age of Reason." Writers were no longer tethered to the strictures of either the church or the state. Their books addressed a wide range of previously banned topics, and readers waited eagerly for the volumes to come off the presses.

In England, writers such as John Locke composed treatises about the proper form of government, and in France, writers like Voltaire were carving out careers as journalists—social commentators who cared little for the suppressive tactics of the clergy and the crown. To publish books of this nature, and make a living at it, would have been unthinkable a century earlier. Voltaire's books—even by today's standards—are acerbic and witty observations of society. They were immensely popular at the time he wrote them, and remain so to this day. *Candide*, one of Voltaire's most famous works, was published in Geneva in 1759. But international copyright was nonexistent, and pirated copies would no doubt undermine any potential financial benefit Voltaire hoped to receive. To circumvent this problem, his publishers sent 1,000 copies of the book to Paris, and hundreds of others to Amsterdam, London, and Brussels. Booksellers in each of these cities agreed to put the work up for sale on the same date, making it much more difficult for pirates to obtain a copy in advance of the work's legal appearance.

Perhaps the highest literary achievement of Enlightenment thinkers was production of the *Encyclopédie*. Considered to be a summary of all knowledge to date, this twenty-eight-volume work, originally printed in folio, was started in 1751 and completed in 1772. The French philosopher and writer Denis Diderot was its leading editor, as well as a contributor.

Under his supervision over 70,000 articles were written and 2,800 plates engraved. There were entries on religion, law, literature, the sciences, arts and crafts, philosophy, military science, and agriculture. In an effort to be both comprehensive and accurate, Diderot and others spent time with artisans of all stripes, learning about leatherworking, papermaking, and the craft of designing jewelry, among other trades. Other contributors focused on the physical, mathematical, and life sciences, producing articles on Newtonian dynamics, natural history, and calculus.

This work, staggering in its breadth of knowledge, was sold by subscription. The first few editions of the book came out in elaborate folio volumes, suited to the initial readership that included noblemen, lawyers, and clergy and royal administrators. By 1754, over 4,000 people had subscribed to the work (none of them with any sense for how long the project would take to complete) and those numbers only increased with each subsequent edition. Moreover, the fourth and fifth editions were printed in quarto and octavo, respectively, which made the work smaller and more affordable for the average book consumer. And consume they would: between 1777 and 1782, print runs of over 8,500 quarto editions, and 5,500 octavo editions were recorded. In these smaller formats the *Encyclopédie* constituted thirty volumes, with three volumes devoted solely to the plates.

Publishers worked overtime to ensure the *Encyclopédie* was promoted across Europe. Bookshops were given flyers to post and prospectuses to display, and local newspapers advertised its sale (Darnton 1979, 265).

Universally popular and utterly comprehensive, the *Encyclopédie* was emblematic of the Enlightenment way of thinking. Emphasis throughout the work was placed on man's reason, with religious orthodoxy relegated to the ranks of the mystical and superstitious. Naturally, not everyone read this with favor. Among those readers who found Diderot's efforts heretical and dangerous were the Jesuits, the King's Council, the General Assembly of the Clergy, and Parisian city officials, all of whom denounced the work. In 1759, it was placed on the official Index of Forbidden Books, from which position it only gained in popularity, as banned books often did. But those who shirked the condemnations of the clergy and elected to read the *Encyclopédie* found themselves immersed in the greatest book—or set of books—printed in the Enlightenment. The spirit of the age was captured in its volumes.

One volume of the *Encyclopédie* was devoted to trades and industry. Here, the intricacies of papermaking, printing, and binding were explored, with technical drawings that illuminated the smallest details of punches, molds, type, forms, and every other component that went into producing a printed book. The explanation was as comprehensive as the engravings were beautiful, even if the neatness of the scenes—a spotless printing shop, a placid bindery, and a handful of stoically attentive workers—belies the true nature of printing houses in this era. It seems probable that they were rowdy work places. Robert Darnton, who has carefully studied the eighteenth-century printing shops, has cataloged the slang found in print-shop manuals and records. He has found words for "noisiness, horseplay, pub-crawling, drunkenness, brawls, indebtedness, absenteeism and unemployment." This is good evidence that the printing scenes in the *Encyclopédie* were idealized. Even so, the illustrations, combined with the narrative accounts of the craft, remain accurate and offer valuable insight into the workings of these shops.

France's period of Enlightenment came to an abrupt end in 1789 with the onset of the French Revolution, a social and political upheaval that ultimately undermined much of the Enlightenment's philosophizing about human nature, and challenged the age's optimism. But the technology of books stood above such regional conflicts, and its development continued steadily. On the eve of the nineteenth century, with literacy expanding and the book market steadily increasing, print technology advanced in a critical way.

In Basel, William Haas was working on a press that was stronger than the traditional wooden press used since Gutenberg's era. Haas decided to build a press that was partially made from iron. The wooden platen and beds in

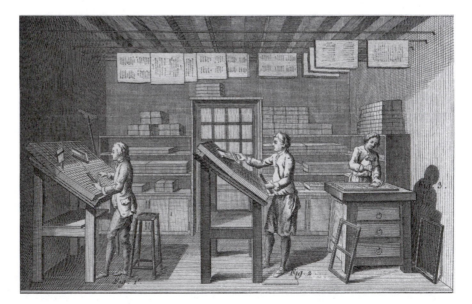

Image of an idealized print shop, from Denis Diderot's French Enlightenment work, *Encyclopédie*. Courtesy of the Burndy Library, Cambridge, Massachusetts.

presses were subjected to extreme forces with each impression. By making them from iron, Haas determined—in 1772—that his press would both yield a better impression and last longer. In 1800, an Englishman followed up on this idea by building a press entirely from iron. These were the most significant changes in printing technology since the initial Mainz development of moveable type, and they would usher in an age of rapid advance in the technology of books and printing. In the next century, the Industrial Revolution would reach its height, first in England and subsequently throughout Europe. It would mark the beginning of modernity for historians, and a new life for books.

5

Maturity: Books in the Age of Automation, 1800–1900

◆

INTRODUCTION: THE EVE OF THE NINETEENTH CENTURY

In the seventeenth and eighteenth centuries, the individuals involved in all aspects of book production—the midwives—saw their roles shifting and evolving. The dynamics of publishing changed, the role of the author was augmented, and the craftsmen printing books tried to keep pace with readers' growing demands. Books had moved out of Europe into the colonies. There, they contributed indirectly to colonial revolutions, and books once produced in the home countries by colonial powers were, by 1800, being printed abroad in newly independent nations. Yet, as the Sun set on the eighteenth century, the print shop operated in much the same way as it had in Gutenberg's era. To be sure, there were advances in typecasting techniques, and both printers and illustrators consistently worked to improve the quality of their images, but on the whole the operation remained largely unchanged.

The same was not true in the following century. Beginning in the nineteenth century, changes to books and book production took place at a rapid clip. Major innovations were introduced in every facet of the printing operation: typecasting, composition, inking, impression, and binding. By the end of the century, a web of integrated machines was producing books and other printed materials at rates that would have been unimaginable in the days of hand-composition and impression.

A host of factors led to this change. First, the nineteenth century saw the Industrial Revolution take hold across Europe. Beginning with the earliest steam-powered engines of Thomas Newcomen and James Watt, a series of technologies emerged that turned small-scale cottage industries into large, organized factories. Automation became the paradigm of efficiency, and a culture of tinkerers and inventors—in both Europe and the United States—sought to apply mechanical power to every kind of production, not the least of which was printing. Books, like textiles or tools, could be produced more quickly and cheaply with the help of machines.

The mechanization of book production was also encouraged by explosive growth in the market for books. Educational reforms across Europe had created a whole new class of readers, resulting in a corresponding increase in the demand for reading material. And it was not just primers or children's books they sought. Adults clamored for books: popular and educational works, fiction and nonfiction, and news, both local and foreign. By the nineteenth century, newspapers were firmly woven into the cultural fabric, their circulation stimulated by the expanding audience of curious readers. Indeed, it was this mounting demand for newspapers that drove much of the period's technological innovation. Unlike the production of books, printing the news was a time-sensitive business. Printers were pressured to develop quicker methods of setting type and making impressions. In the end, it was the newspaper industry that pushed the technology forward. Books were the beneficiaries of these advances.

ON THE EVE OF AUTOMATION

In the years leading up to the mechanization of book production, incremental improvements in printing presses set the stage for advances in automation that were to come. The first of these was the introduction of the iron press. Although numerous individuals contributed to the design and construction of this press, credit is generally given to an English nobleman and amateur scientist, Charles Stanhope, Third Earl Stanhope (1753–1816). His iron press, invented in 1803, looked much like Gutenberg's original wooden press, but the "Stanhope"—as it was called—improved the mechanism of the screw lever (the handle that pressmen pulled). Both the iron structure and the improved lever allowed for greater stability when making the impression. Now, printers could use a larger platen, thereby increasing the impression area. Earlier printers had typically used two pulls of the press lever to print one large sheet of paper, which would eventually be folded into folio, quarto, or octavo leaves. The old platen covered a surface area of about 49×39 cm, while Stanhope's press eventually allowed for impression over a 98×58 cm area, thereby eliminating the double pull required of pressmen (Gaskell 1995, 199). Following the pressman's pull of the lever, the platen automatically returned to the raised position, drawn up by a counterweight.

Stanhope's invention improved both the efficiency and the quality of the press. The advance was immediately recognized by printers, and by the 1820s the iron press had largely replaced older wooden presses. Its utility was also quickly seized upon by the burgeoning community of newspaper printers, including *The Times* of London, which purchased "a battalion" of Stanhope presses soon after their introduction. By 1811, these presses were being manufactured in New York, and within a few years, similar models were being constructed in Germany and France.

Stanhope's iron press was followed by a series of similar presses, that offered small but valuable improvements in design and performance. In 1813, Philadelphia printer George Clymer developed a press known as the "Columbian," the first iron press used in the Americas. Clymer's main innovation was in the power train: whereas earlier pressmen lowered the platen onto the chase with a screw mechanism (thereby applying pressure to the type), the Columbian replaced the screw with a series of small levers. This was advantageous because it eliminated the slight twisting motion of the platen as the screw turned, which could result in smeared ink. Clymer's press, which could be purchased for $400, was used by printers for over one hundred years.

London printer Richard Cope followed Clymer's example, introducing the Columbian to Britain and then inventing his own press in 1822, called the "Albion." This press became famous for the toggle mechanism it used to lower the platen. Unlike the screw and the lever system, Cope's toggle straightened to depress the platen, which was then returned to its starting position by a spring. Cope later replaced the spring with a counterweight, which pulled the platen back into position.

Other iron presses followed Cope's, each making some improvement to the quality of typography. Though they were welcomed by printers in Europe and America for their stability and efficiency, they still resembled—in broad form and function—the first presses used in Mainz in the fifteenth century.

As historians of technology have shown, webs of technology—interrelated machines or operations—tend to develop as a group. One has only to look at the development of computer technology to recognize the

George Clymer's Columbian press. Courtesy of the Bancroft Library, University of California, Berkeley.

truth of this. Each innovation has a tendency to foster evolution in other, related, areas. This is nowhere better exemplified than in the development of print technologies in the nineteenth century. As the wooden press advanced to its iron form, other aspects of the printing process were improved as well. One such advancement was a printing technique called "stereotyping." With this method, a mold was made of an entire page of set type, thereby preserving the page for future printings. This not only spared the compositor the effort of resetting multiple pages, but also conserved the type itself—which would otherwise become worn down with each use. As the cast of a page deteriorated, a new cast could be made from the original mold, instead of resetting the entire page. In a sense, the stereotype worked similar to a block book, printing the entire page—type plus illustration—from a unified image.

Printers had experimented with stereotyping as early as 1700. For example, the German printer Johann Müller made plates for several of his books between 1700 and 1718 (Gaskell 1995, 201). In 1804, a year after inventing the iron press, Lord Stanhope developed a stereotyping method that utilized plaster to create a mold of the page. Into this mold, molten lead was poured, resulting in a full-page copy of the original bed of type. This was treated just as a traditional type bed would be: it was inked and slid beneath the platen. The great advantage of this method was that reprints were simple to produce; the printer just went back to the plaster matrices and made the needed impressions. For books like the Bible, or classics, where multiple print runs could be expected, stereotyping looked like a wonderful tool.

But early stereotyping efforts ran into both practical and cultural barriers. First, the method required an investment on the part of printers to train the stereotyper. This expense alone deterred some printers. Moreover, the plaster that formed against the type left residue when removed, and it was tedious to pick out the plaster from the crevices of type. More damage could be done cleaning up the type than would have been done with additional impressions. Finally, there were labor issues. Compositors were strongly opposed to stereotyping, since it infringed upon their trade and threatened to reduce the amount of available work. Books that promised to appear in multiple editions (e.g., Bibles, primers) provided compositors with guaranteed income, but the stereotype plates rendered needless the task of resetting type. Compositors in England organized themselves in 1834, forming "The London Union Company of Compositors," in an effort to preserve their livelihood. For all of these reasons, use of stereotyping was fairly limited in the eighteenth century.

Labor problems were gradually solved by an often-bitter process of socioeconomic adjustment. Technically, however, the solution to the problems of a plaster stereotype mold was found in the development of a paper material called "flong"—tissue and blotting papers mixed together in a dampened state and laid over type. When dried, it would take the impression of type without causing any damage to the original form, being easily removed from the face of the type. Flong molds could also be made to cover a much larger surface area than plaster molds did.

In 1816, printers further advanced the stereotyping technique by creating cylindrical stereotypes that could be inked and rolled over the paper, instead of being slid beneath a flat platen. As more rotary presses were introduced (see below) this advance became invaluable.

Another useful process was electrotyping, developed simultaneously (though independently) in 1839 by Russian, English, and American printers. The famous American publisher *Harper's* issued a book in 1855 about the printing process, *The Harper Establishment; or, How the Story Books are Made*. This is their description of electrotyping:

> It has been discovered within a few years that if a liquid contains any metal in solution, an arrangement may be made of electric wires, so that, under the influence of the electric current brought by the wires, the particles of the metal in the solution will be slowly deposited upon any metallic plate which may be immersed in the liquid.

Based on this principle, which we now call electroplating, passage of electrical current through a metal-bearing solution will cause particles of the metal—say copper—to separate from the water, so that the metal can adhere to a conductive mold. This mold, usually of graphite-coated wax, was made in a manner similar to stereotype molds: the wax was heated and pressed onto the form that contained the type. The wax mold was dipped in the electrified fluid, whereupon,

> the deposition of copper all over the surface of the mold immediately commences. The particles find their way into all the interstices of the [mold], and into the very finest lines of the engraving, so as to reproduce exactly every touch and lineament, however delicate and fine, of the engraved work.

When enough copper had adhered to the wax mold to create a sufficiently thick copy, the mold was pulled away, leaving a thin copper reproduction of the original type. A layer of lead was applied to the copperplate to reinforce it for printing. This method created precise, clean copies, both of type and of engraved images. Moreover, the copperplate was significantly lighter than a standard form with type (one-fifth the weight, according to *Harper's*), making it much easier for the printer to handle.

THE NEW TECHNOLOGY OF BOOKS: AUTOMATION IN THE NINETEENTH CENTURY

Book production involves a series of interrelated technologies and processes, beginning with typecasting, moving on to composition and impression, and ending with collating and binding. Automation obviously led to production efficiencies in each of these areas, but it was hardly welcomed by the men who produced books. In much the same way scribes resisted the newly developed moveable type, or illuminators fought the introduction of multicolored illustrations from a press, the craftsmen of the early nineteenth-century shop organized themselves in an effort to defend against new technologies.

Initially, printing shops that attempted to break away from traditional methods and employ automation risked retaliation. Disgruntled workers, lamenting the loss of their livelihood, threatened to destroy equipment, or at the least abandon any printing shop that was using it. This posed a serious dilemma for a master printer. Even if one aspect of printing was automated, he or she would still need employees to carry out a range of other tasks. Losing them all—and suffering the financial blow of destroyed equipment—over the transition to machine-powered equipment was hardly worth the savings the new technology brought to the shop. In both England and France, expensive typecasting machines were purchased by master printers, only to be destroyed by the workers in protest (Steinberg 1959, 277). This reality led many shops to delay adoption of available technology.

Industrial Presses: From Iron to Steam

The first aspect of printing to be automated was the press itself. If the transition from wooden to iron presses was significant, the shift from human to steam-powered presses was a quantum leap. Europeans, caught up in the fervor of the Industrial Revolution of the nineteenth century, were eagerly looking for new applications for steam power, including the printing press.

In the early nineteenth century, the German printer Fredrich König began a series of attempts to improve upon the printing press. Ultimately, he hoped to build an automated press based on steam technology. His story was a drama of innovation and frustration, but eventually his repeated attempts to improve the technology bore fruit. The impact König had on the technology of the book is hard to overstate.

König started work on the press in 1802, and after several failed—or less than efficient—efforts, he built a press that differed slightly from the commonly used platen presses. Instead of setting the bed of type beneath a platen that was lowered down onto it, König's press had a moveable carriage

A single-cylinder press, where the impression is made by a revolving cylinder that rolls over a bed of type. Courtesy of the Bancroft Library, University of California, Berkeley.

(on which the bed of type was set) that received ink by rolling beneath an inking apparatus. The impression was then made by the application of pressure from a standard platen.

Perhaps because it differed little from the presses in use, investors were reluctant to acknowledge the value of König's technique and offer funding for its development. König looked outside of Germany, where he had lived and worked, but found little more than a dead-end position at the Imperial Russian Press. He, therefore, turned his attention to England, a decision he later reflected upon unambiguously:

> The well-known fact, that almost every invention seeks, as it were, refuge in England, and is there brought to perfection . . . seems to indicate that the Continent has yet to learn from her [England] the best manner of encouraging the mechanical arts. I had my full share in the ordinary disappointments of Continental projectors; and after having lost in Germany and Russia upwards of two years in fruitless applications, I at last resorted to England. (Letter in *The Times*, December 8, 1814)

In England, König enlisted the support of Thomas Bensley, an established London printer, as he continued to work on his press. But the innovation stalled, and König—in concert with partner Andrew Bauer (also a German printer who had moved to England)—sought to reconceptualize the entire press. Rather than build on the traditional platen/type-bed model, the pair sought to utilize cylinders in their press, reducing all the horizontal and vertical actions of the press to rotary actions.

Initial efforts in this direction led to a patent in 1810 for a platen press with two key innovations: the inking of the type was done mechanically by revolving cylinders, and the entire press was moved by a steam engine. König wrote:

> After many obstructions and delays, the first printing machine was completed exactly upon the plan which I have described in the specification of my first patent . . . The sheet of the new Annual Register for 1810 'Principal Occurrence,' 3000 copies, was printed with it; and is, I have no doubt, the first part of a book ever printed with a machine. (Letter in *The Times*, December 8, 1814)

A series of improvements followed for König's press, each one moving him closer to his vision of a steam-powered rotary press. Patents in 1811, 1813, and 1814 testify to the decisive moments when another step was taken. The last of these patents protected his design for a press that had a main cylinder, around which blank paper was wrapped—the paper being fed from a continual supply known as "web fed." This paper-covered cylinder would rotate over a bed of type, transferring the image to the paper as it revolved. Finally, the paper was ejected from the cylinder and fed back through the same system to receive a second impression on the back side. It was not simultaneous two-sided printing, but the speed of the process nevertheless made it efficient. Thus, in 1814, König had invented a single-cylinder, web-fed, steam-powered press.

Among the many advantages of König's press was the need for less force to make an impression, due to the rolling of the cylinder across type. Imagine trying to flatten out a lump of dough with a large flat surface versus a rolling pin: the latter requires significantly less force and proves far more efficient because the force needs only to be concentrated on the point of contact of the roller with the dough. So too, with a bed of type beneath a rotating cylinder. This reduction in force required for impression made it all the more practical to automate König's machine. The impression cylinders were powered by a 2-horsepower steam engine, removing the need for a pressman to pull a lever all day. The ink was applied automatically, the bed of type was pushed beneath the cylinder, and the impression was transferred automatically to a sheet of paper sitting atop the type.

Whereas Stanhope's iron handpress produced approximately 250 impressions per hour (or 125 two-sided sheets), König's cylinder press was capable of meeting the demands of newspaper printing, with over 1,000 pages an hour. Again, though, this automation was not welcomed by everyone. Workers in print shops feared being displaced by machines that worked ten times faster with only two operators. Mechanics, machinists, and founders involved with building König's presses signed agreements not to disclose any details of the invention before it was installed in print shops, both to protect the details of manufacture and to forestall labor unrest in the shops for which these new presses were destined.

In 1814, the single-cylinder press—developed with newspapers in mind—was adopted by *The Times* of London, the widest circulating paper in the world at the time. Fearing retribution from its workers, who had threatened destruction to the machines, *The Times* publisher, John Walter II, had secretly installed the new König presses in a building next door to *The Times* office. Only when the daily paper appeared on November 29 did pressmen discover it had been printed by a steam-powered press. The paper boldly announced its use of the invention in terms that proclaimed a new era in print technology:

> Our Journal of this day present to the Public the practical result of the greatest improvement connected with printing since the discovery of the art itself. The reader of this paragraph now holds in his hand one of the many thousand impression of *The Times* newspaper which were taken off last night by a mechanical apparatus. A system of machinery almost organic has been devised and arranged, which, while it relieves the human frame of its most laborious efforts in printing, far exceeds all human powers in rapidity and dispatch. That the magnitude of the invention may be justly appreciated by its effects, we shall inform the public, that after the letters are placed by the compositors, and enclosed in what is called the forme, little more remains for man to do than to attend upon and to watch this unconscious agent in its operations.

And what about the pressmen, soon to be out of work? *The Times* offered only this:

> There is another class of men from whom we receive dark and anonymous threats of vengeance if we persevere in the use of this machine. These are the Pressmen. They well know . . . that such menace is thrown away upon us. There is nothing that we will not do to assist and serve those whom we have discharged. They themselves can see the greater rapidity and precision with which the paper is printed. What right have they to make us print it slower and worse for their supposed benefit? A little reflection, indeed, would show them that it is neither in their power

nor in ours to stop a discovery now made, if it is beneficial to mankind . . .
(*The Times*, December 3, 1814)

Though König remained involved in press production, improving on his first models, his ideas were quickly built upon by a number of inventors and printers, few of whom honored König's patents (including his long-time partner Bensley, who took credit for much of König's work). In 1816, Edward Cowper, a British printer, patented his technique for creating curved stereotype plates using the plaster method. By slowly heating and bending the metal mold, he showed how to wrap it around a cylinder. This ushered in the age of the rotary press, where the impression was no longer made by a cylinder pressing against a bed of type, but by pressure applied to a cylinder of type.

The next challenge was a "perfected" machine—one that would print both sides of a sheet of paper without being handled by a pressman. Cowper set to work on this, teaming up with Augustus Applegarth, in 1820, to invent a two-cylinder press that printed two-sided pages by flipping the sheet of paper through a second set of cylinders to expose the blank side to type. The result was 700–1,000 two-sided, or perfected, sheets per hour (Gaskell 1995, 262). In 1828, Cowper and Applegarth bettered their achievement with a four-cylinder press that printed 4,000 sheets per hour. Theirs was followed by a type-revolving press capable of producing 8,000 sheets per hour. The days of Gutenberg's wooden handpress were suddenly a distant memory.

Use of these rotary presses was not limited to the world of newspapers. In 1826, König's press was adapted to the mass production of books by F. A. Brockhaus, a German publisher. The speed and economy of these presses—which lowered book costs by 25 percent—ultimately rendered them invaluable to printers, whose profit margins on books had traditionally been narrow.

Compared to newspaper printers, though, book printers were slow to adopt these presses. In the 1830s, powered platen presses were still being used by most book printers. These were automated presses, but instead of adopting a rotary motion, they continued to press a platen onto a bed of type with the paper in between to receive the impression. The Adams Power Press, patented by Isaac Adams in 1830, was the most commonly used platen press in the United States through most of the nineteenth century. Capable of 500 impressions per hour, it was not as efficient as the rotary presses of the day, but it was valued by book printers for the high-quality impressions it made. It was not until after 1870 that rotary machines replaced the platen presses almost universally. By the turn of the twentieth

The Adams Power Press, widely used in the United States in the mid-nineteenth century for book printing. Courtesy of the Bancroft Library, University of California, Berkeley.

century, with the exception of certain fine-book presses, rotary presses were ubiquitous in the bookmaking trade (Gaskell 1995, 254).

Papermaking

In order to keep pace with the ability to print more quickly, other facets of printing had to be automated as well. Among these was the manufacture of paper, which had typically been the costliest—and in many ways the slowest—aspect of bookmaking. Beginning in 1798, Nicolas Louis Robert made great strides toward the mechanical production of paper. He created an Endless Wire Papermaking Machine that produced one long roll of paper (up to 50 feet in length), as opposed to individual sheets.

Several steps were involved in his papermaking process. First, wet, pulpy material from a vat was deposited on a vibrating wire belt. The agitation served to dry the pulp and to cross the pulp fibers, creating a random weave that would render the paper stronger. Next, the pulp passed through a series of stacked rollers that squeezed out additional moisture and flattened the material. The pulp emerged from these rollers onto a second belt—lined with felt—which carried it to a second set of hot rollers. After receiving this second press, the paper was given a smooth finish with a heated press. What came off the assembly line was a continuous sheet of paper, called wove paper, which lacked both chain lines and watermarks—hallmarks of handmade paper.

Robert's invention removed the need for a man to constantly attend a vat of pulp; it also increased the rate of paper production. Shortly after completing his invention, Robert attempted to sell the patent to his French employer, the well-known printer St. Leger Didot, but the latter could not afford the payments. The papermaking technology was then taken to England, where, in April 1801, it earned both the approval of printers and an English patent (#2487). Robert's patent protected the rights to a papermaking machine that was ten times faster than any previous papermaking process. In turn, prices dropped rapidly. What had always been the most expensive material in book production was now about 30 percent cheaper. The production of paper in England went from 10,000 tons per year to over 100,000 tons. By 1900, the United Kingdom would produce well over half a million tons of paper.

Papermakers in England were naturally threatened by the potential of this machine, which, in 1800, prompted them to organize as a group, becoming the Original Society of Papermakers (OSP), a body that existed until 1982. But their union could barely slow down the inevitable.

Robert's paper machine was improved upon in subsequent years by several individuals, but it was the financial backing of the Fourdrinier brothers that made it practicable and widely available. They procured the rights to production of what was subsequently known as the Fourdrinier Paper Machine, and marketed it in Europe and the United States. In 1827, one of their machines was installed in Saugerties, New York, and within two years, American printers had built a model of their own.

With a continuous roll of paper easily produced, it was only logical to link that technology with an automated press. The first step toward this end was taken in 1846 by the New York inventor Richard Hoe. Building on the idea of König's rotary press, Hoe made a simple—but key—structural change. Instead of having the paper wrapped around the cylinder, waiting to roll across inked type on a horizontal bed, Hoe wrapped the type itself around the cylinder, which was positioned horizontally. He was able to do this not with individual pieces of type, but by employing stereotyping techniques. A thin plate with lines of text could be wrapped around the cylinder, the letters standing up in relief. This cylinder of type which was surrounded by four impression cylinders would be inked. Paper was then hand-fed into each of the four cylinders, every page receiving the impression from the main, inked cylinder.

Once built, it was known as the Hoe Type-Revolving Machine and was quickly adopted by printers—principally newspaper printers—in the United States, earning R. Hoe & Co. a healthy profit. In the 1861 edition of Thomas Adams's *Typographia; or, The Printer's instructor*, Hoe's single-cylinder press was deemed one of the most important innovations in the history of book production: "So excellent is its performance, that in every extensive printing establishment it has almost entirely superceded the hand press" (Adams 1861, 271).

The marriage of the rotary press and the Fourdrinier paper machine was arranged by William Bullock, a Philadelphia inventor who, in 1863, received U.S. patent (#38200) for his web-fed press. This machine-powered press utilized curved stereotype plates around the cylinders, an automatic paper-feeding system, and two-sided printing. It was, in short, the culmination of myriad processes that had been developed since the start of the nineteenth century, and its value was immediately shown in its production capability of 10,000 perfected sheets per hour (Kilgour 1998, 119).

Papermaking also underwent significant changes when, in 1843, the German Friedrich Gottlob Keller found a way to make paper from wood pulp, instead of the commonly used, but expensive, rags. The shift to wood pulp meant that paper became even cheaper to produce, and places with an abundance of forests especially profited. The United States emerged an early leader in paper production, thanks to its dense forests.

Automated Composition

Next in line for automation in the production of the printed book were typecasting and composition. It was the New Yorker David Bruce who, in 1838, came up with a method of creating pieces of type mechanically, attesting once again to the United States' active role in the development of printing technologies. His automated typecaster brought a mold up to a spigot where molten metal was pushed into it. The mold then swung away from the spigot, expelling the piece of already-hardened type. Bruce's machine fabricated between 12,000 and 20,000 pieces of type each day, compared to the 3,000 to 7,000 pieces that were typically cast with hand molds. By the late nineteenth century, a rotary typecaster that used 100 molds to create 60,000 pieces of type an hour had been developed.

The next step for printers seeking to streamline their operation was to mechanize composition. The careful setting of type according to a manuscript was a significantly more complex process than that of making type or creating impressions. Two kinds of composing machines were used in the nineteenth century, cold-metal and hot-metal. The cold-metal machines were built with the individual pieces of type already cast and stacked in magazines or cartridges. Pressing a button could trigger a door, opening the shaft with the letter "b" in it. The "b" would then fall down from the shaft into position on a line. Another button—pressed by an operator—would release the door for the shaft containing "o" and another for "y" followed.

On a line, then, the pieces of type to spell "boy" were assembled. Instead of a composer grabbing the type himself and arranging it on a composing stick, the machine dropped type into place. The earliest of these typesetting machines went into operation in 1840. Frenchmen J. H. Young and A. Delcambre patented their "Pianotype" machine, which required three men to operate it: one to run the keyboard, another to justify the lines, and a third to restore type to the machine after use. Working efficiently, the Pianotype could set 6,000 characters (letters and spaces) in one hour, double of what a compositor could do by hand. Further efforts in the mid-nineteenth century led to the 1857 patent of Robert Hattersley, whose composition machines were used by printers up until the First World War. To be sure, these cold-metal machines marked an improvement over manual methods, but enormous supplies of type had to be stacked in the magazines, and each line still had to be justified by hand. The process remained cumbersome.

What was needed was a machine that could both cast and compose type for printing, and all the better if the lines came out justified. In considering this technological problem, it occurred to the Milwaukee printer Linn Boyd Benton that a machine to create punches was a first step. In 1885 Benton received U.S. patent (#327855) for his "Pantograph," a mechanical engraver that could cut both the punches and the matrices. Richard Huss clearly identified the advantage of Benton's machine:

> With the developing composition-matrix machines, many duplicates of matrices were required for each machine, multiplied by the number of machines sold. Consequently, a broken punch was a great problem—an intolerable one—because of the great time required to re-cut the punch using hand methods. Benton's machine minimized this problem by making it possible to mechanically duplicate a damaged punch in a short time. And thus the great pressure of production of matrices for composing machines was moved to the punch. (Huss 1985, 10)

Benton's pantographic engraver was picked up by Ottmar Mergenthaler (1854–1899), a German American who built a prototype of his revolutionary "Linotype" machine in 1886. The same year his machine was installed at the *New York Tribune*, where publisher Whitelaw Reid reportedly exclaimed, "Ottmar, you've done it again! A line o' type!"

The one remaining challenge to the automated production and composition of type was the technological hurdle of casting type on demand. Mergenthaler solved this problem in 1889 by employing Benton's Pantograph technology. In a "Report of the Board of Directors" of January 21, 1888, the Brooklyn-based Mergenthaler Printing Company wrote:

> The matrix problem has been solved. The matrices are by no means perfect yet, but the defects are largely due to defective dies [punches]; and by contract recently completed with Benton, Waldo & Co., of Milwaukee, for the mechanical cutting of these dies, it is believed that absolute accuracy in the reproduction of the best styles of types can now be secured. (Huss 1985, 5)

Where cold-metal compositors stacked actual pieces of type in a magazine, Mergenthaler's Linotype had matrices stacked in a magazine. An operator sat at a keypad that contained ninety characters (fifteen columns of six keys), each key controlling a specific matrix. When the operator depressed a button for the letter "b," the matrix for "b" was dropped into position on a belt. Once an entire line was typed, the operator pulled a lever, which justified the line of matrices by putting spaces between words. The resulting line of justified type was called a "slug." The slug received molten metal, which hardened immediately, thereby casting an entire line of type at once. Each line of type moved to a galley, and a full galley was a page ready for inking and printing. Once the type had issued from the matrices, they rotated back into position in the magazine.

The Linotype machine effectively handled the first half of the printing operation: typecasting, composition, justification, and the setting of type into forms. It initially composed 6,000 characters, or "ens" (a piece of type the width of an "n") per hour, but with improvements and skilled operators, Linotype could produce 10,000 ens per hour, somewhere between four and seven lines of type each minute. Thomas Edison—renowned for his own contributions to technology—called Linotype the "Eighth Wonder of the World." By 1900, over 6,000 Linotype machines were in use; fifteen years later the number exceeded 30,000 worldwide. Though most Linotype machines were operating in newspaper offices, the technology was quickly adopted for book production as well.

After Mergenthaler's initial innovation, he and others improved on the machine's efficiency. His 1892 Simplex Linotype Model 1 became the industry standard, the pattern for over 100,000 Linotype machines built. In 1912, when Mergenthaler's patent expired, other similar machines emerged: the Typograph (used principally to create special slug lines, such as for newspapers), Linograph (a smaller and simplified form of Linotype), and Intertype (rebuilt and improved Linotype machines).

Similar in function to the Linotype machine was the Monotype, first produced by Tolbert Lanston (1844–1913) in the early 1890s. Unlike Linotype, Monotype required two separate machines—a keyboard and a caster—which were operated in two different rooms. The keyboard had between

Two components of a Lanston Monotype Machine: a keyboard and a caster. Courtesy of the Bancroft Library, University of California, Berkeley.

150 and 250 keys. When an operator pressed a key, a burst of compressed air punched a hole on a spool—or ribbon—of paper. The position of the hole on the ribbon correlated to the type that would be produced. After a line was typed and the respective perforations made, the machine punched in the appropriate amount of spacing to justify the line, and a new line was started.

When all the holes for a given page are punched, the ribbon—full of holes—was taken into the casting room and fed into the machine containing the matrix case. This case consisted of a rectangular frame that held 225 matrices. Air passing through the punched holes in the ribbon moved the matrix case in four directions (up, down, left, right) to correctly position the appropriate matrix cartridge. The proper letter was then released, the spool advanced, and the next hole determined the next matrix to be dropped into place. When all the matrices were in place, an entire galley of type was cast at once.

In 1916, the Lanston Monotype Company published *The Monotype System: A Book for Owners and Operators of Monotype*. In superlative tones, the title page to this book heralded the new technology: "The word Monotype means much more than the name of a machine, it includes a complete system of composing-room efficiency based on the work of the Monotype as both a composing machine and as a type and rule caster."

This was the age of high-speed book production and the Monotype Corporation, which was training people to use its machines in a mere two months, placed itself squarely in the center of a printing revolution. However, the company's ambitious vision and bold language was tempered by an awareness that their machines threatened the livelihood of hand compositors. To successfully enter the printing market, they had to convince this group of skilled craftsmen that their composition skills would not be neglected. Thus, the preface to the Monotype manual offered the following assurance:

> The Monotype is the only composing machine that recognizes the existence of the hand compositor. It is not built on the impossible theory that the compositor can be driven from the printing industry; instead it provides the means for increasing efficiency and making his work highly profitable to his employer.

However hollow this promise proved in the end, it demonstrates the power that organized labor had, and the need for companies to maneuver sensitively if they hoped to establish a foothold in the business.

The overall effect of the automated composing machines was that the cost of type went down significantly, and therefore the price of books dropped. A corollary effect was the standardization of type sizes in the industry. Moves to standardize type had been afoot for a century, but it was the mass production of type that forced the issue. In 1886 the United States Type Founders' Association adopted the American Points System. This was based on an earlier French model developed by François-Ambroise Didot and Pierre Simon Fournier, both of whom used the "pica" as a measurement. The American system, also adopted by Britain, used the pica by dividing it into twelfths, each twelfth called a "point." One point is equivalent to .013837 ($\frac{1}{72}$) of an inch. The standard measure of a piece of type became the number of points it had.

By the turn of the century, Linotype and Monotype were popular in both the United States and Europe, though European book printers preferred Monotype, feeling that Linotype produced an inferior product (this despite the fact that American printers managed to produce high-quality books with it). The machines themselves were operated by two ranks of workers: machine minders (some of whom had done an apprenticeship) and machine boys—many as young as eleven years old and most with no experience in the printing industry. The specialized skill-set required of the seventeenth- and eighteenth-century compositors was rendered obsolete in the face of this new technology.

Illustration and Lithography

The great strides taken in printing text in the nineteenth century were matched by advances in image-printing techniques. While the printing of Gutenberg's era had almost all been done in relief—with raised images and letters—and the illustrators of the seventeenth and eighteenth centuries utilized intaglio methods, the nineteenth-century technique, known as lithography, shunned both. Instead, lithographic printing—otherwise known as planographic printing—was done on a flat surface. In lithography, image transmission depends not on mechanical actions, but on the chemical properties of attraction between oils, and the lack of affinity between oil and water.

One of the earliest contributions to lithography came from the German playwright-turned-printer Alois Senefelder. Indeed, it was Senefelder's disappointment at not finding a publisher for a play he wrote that spurred his attempt to print it himself. In the last years of the eighteenth century he experimented with a technique whereby images could be created on stone—such as limestone, which has a coarse surface—and reproduced by using an oil and water combination. Central to his method was the chemical relationship mentioned above. Senefelder drew an image with an oily substance—like a crayon—and then washed the stone surface with water. The water remained on the surface of the stone everywhere except where he had written with the crayon. He then applied a hydrophobic ink to the stone. The ink was repelled by the watery parts of the stone but adhered to the oily marks from the crayon, which were water-free. With the image on the stone now inked, Senefelder placed a piece of paper over the stone, thereby transferring the image to paper. Because the process was fundamentally based on chemical affinities, he called it "chemical printing."

In recounting his invention, Senefelder was emphatic about the thoughtfulness of his process, denying rumors of coincidence or chance in making his discovery. After detailing his experiments with the process, Senefelder (1911) wrote, "I have told all these things fully in order to prove to the reader that I did not invent stone-printing through lucky accident, but that I arrived at it by a way pointed out by industrious thought."

Senefelder created a press in 1817 that both wet the plate and inked it automatically, making the process practicable for mass production of images. Because the printing surface was flat, lithographic printing needed significant pressure from the press. A thicker ink was also required, so that it would better adhere to the oily image. Senefelder's lithographic method was made public in his 1818 work *Complete Manual of Stone Printing*, and he was appointed Royal Inspector of Lithography for Bavaria.

Color lithography—known as chromolithography—was also made possible by using the same image on multiple stones, but inking the stones in different colors. Thus, the paper for a multicolor image would first be impressed against a stone with black ink, then against one with red, and so forth, until all the colors had been impressed on the paper. Aligning the images for each impression proved difficult, but if the paper was set correctly for each subsequent impression, the result was a truly sharp and beautiful image.

Lithography, and the concept of planographic printing in general, had a tremendous impact not just on illustration, but on printing itself. Lithographic plates originally made of stone were soon composed of more flexible metals, such as aluminum and zinc. Plates of plastic and paper were also developed for use with rotary printing machines. In 1851, the Scotch printing firm of Maclure & Macdonald brought the first cylinder-lithograph printing machine to Britain. By the twentieth century, a planographic method known as offset printing would become the standard technique of book production.

Photography

Subsequent advances in the printing of both images and text were highly influenced by the introduction of photography, and its eventual application to lithography marked an advance in book illustration. In the early nineteenth century, Louis Jacques Mandé Daguerre and Nicephore Niépce were working together on a technique to fix images on a plate by exposing it to certain chemicals. Prior to his partnership with Daguerre, Niépce had successfully made a photograph (of a granary), but his method required over 7 hours of exposure. It was Daguerre who refined Niépce's technique and earned a place in the public's memory. In 1837, the first "Daguerreotype" was made, a positive image on a silver plate that was the antecedent of today's photograph. The *Boston Daily Advertiser* of February 23, 1839, records the invention:

> At a session of the Academy of Sciences, held the 8th of January, M. Arago gave an account of a curious invention lately made by M. Daguerre; for making drawings . . . The new invention is a method of fixing the image permanently on the paper, or making a permanent drawing, by the agency of the light alone; ten or fifteen minutes being amply sufficient for taking any view, though the time varies with the intensity of the light. By this machine M. Daguerre has made accurate drawings of the gallery of the Louvre and of Notre Dame; any object indeed, or any natural appearance may be copied by it—it reproduces the freshness of morning—the brilliancy of noon—the dim twilight and the dullness of a

rainy day. The colours are marked by a gradation of shades similar to aqualuita.

This invention was improved upon by William Henry Fox-Talbot, an Englishman who—just a few weeks after Daguerre's presentation to the Academy of Sciences—came up with his own method wherein the original image was captured on a negative, which required less exposure to light. Positive photos could then be made from the negative, as many times as one liked.

Photography was almost immediately adopted by printers and illustrators, eager to enhance their books with "real" images. As a *New Yorker* editorial of 1839 said, "In the merely imitative walk, and that chiefly for scientific purposes, draughts of machinery, and objects of natural history, the practice of art, as it now exists, will be nearly annihilated."

Anna Atkins's botanical work *British Algae: Cyanotype Impressions*, which contained more than 400 pictures, was the first book to employ this photographic technology. It was published over a period of ten years, beginning in 1843. The word "cyanotype" in the title refers to the process of placing a plant specimen on top of a sheet of chemically treated paper. Exposed to sunlight, the specimen's image forms on the paper with a bright blue hue (called cyan) where the paper was exposed to light, and white where the sunlight was blocked. Atkins's pictures are technically known as photograms, because she did not use a camera—only exposure to light—to create them.

Photographs, images created with a camera, appeared publicly for the first time in Fox-Talbot's *The Pencil of Nature*, published in 1844 by Longmans in London. The book opened with a preface to the reader, highlighting the method by which images were made:

> The plates of the present work are impressed by the agency of Light alone, without any aid whatever from the artist's pencil. They are the sun-pictures themselves, and not, as some persons have imagined, engravings in imitation.

What followed was a series of photographs, of people and places Talbot knew. Lacock Abbey became the first building "that was ever known to have drawn its own picture," Talbot wrote, after including its photograph. A Parisian boulevard, a mound of fruit, and a ladder set against a haystack were also included in the eclectic book, 200 copies of which were sold by subscription.

In 1879, the photograph was incorporated into a method known as "photogravure." Gravure involves an intaglio process: the image is recessed into the surface being used. Photogravure, therefore, allows a photograph to

William Henry Fox-Talbot's photograph of books, which appeared in *The Pencil of Nature*, published in 1844. This was the first printed book to contain photographs. Courtesy of Graphic Arts Collection, Department of Rare Books and Special Collections, Princeton University Library.

be chemically reproduced on a plate. Karl Klic, of Vienna, was able to etch a photographic image into a copperplate. The quality was significantly better than anything produced before, because the fidelity of the photograph was so great. No longer were illustrations just artists' renderings. Instead, reproduction of actual photos represented a higher degree of reality, both subjectively and objectively. Of course, not everyone was eager to adopt the new imaging techniques. A reporter for the *Leipzig City Advertiser* registered his complaint in the first year Daguerreotypes appeared:

> The wish to capture evanescent reflections is not only impossible . . . but the mere desire alone, the will to do so, is blasphemy. God created man in His own image, and no man-made machine may fix the image of God. Is it possible that God should have abandoned His eternal principles, and allowed a Frenchman . . . to give to the world an invention of the Devil?

Yet, even the critic Charles Baudelaire, who worried that photography would supplant or corrupt art, recognized its potential role in preserving important books: "Let [photography] rescue from oblivion those tumbling ruins, those books, prints and manuscripts which time is devouring, precious things whose form is dissolving and which demand a place in the archives of our memory . . ."

In the world of book production, however, the potential of photographic images to complement text was quickly seized upon and implemented. By the mid-1890s, photogravure plates could be rounded, so that the image could be reproduced from a cylindrical copperplate, in which it had been etched. This process was known as "rotogravure."

Packaging and Marketing

With production rates so high, there had to be a practicable way of binding books cheaply. At the turn of the century, most books were still sold unbound, but this would change with the introduction of automatically applied bindings. Cloth bindings had been introduced in 1823 by the Englishman William Pickering. While less sturdy than traditional bindings, they were economical and therefore became increasingly popular. The nineteenth century also saw the introduction of the first book jacket, which appeared on a book entitled *Heath's Keepsake* in 1833. This would become a more common practice by the century's end.

Binding books became significantly easier in 1882 when machine-sewn bindings were used. Essentially, the book's cover was made before the binding was glued on: after the pasteboard had been covered in cloth, the bookblock (the text and any additional leaves) was mechanically glued into the cover. The result was a cheap way of protecting the pages. This made bound books affordable, and therefore readily available for purchase. The majority of books today are bound this way.

LOOKING BACK: THE ART OF FINE PRINTING

Amid the barrage of nineteenth-century printing innovations, the efforts of printers who maintained a strong affection for the book's origins must be acknowledged. In fact, it was only in the face of sweeping technological changes that the notion of a fine-art press could emerge. William Morris's work exemplifies a style of printing that was marginalized, but nevertheless valued, in his industrial century.

Born in 1834 and educated at Oxford, Morris found his calling in design. At an early age he was involved in the design of furniture. He was keenly interested in the relationships between art and environment, and his artistic efforts led Morris to printing. He started the Kelmscott Press in 1891 with the aim of producing books reminiscent of print's earliest centuries. To him, a book was more than a piece of information technology—more than a conduit for the passage of information from page to reader. Rather, books represented artistic opportunities, and Morris's approach to their design was holistic: all aspects had to be thoughtfully developed. The final product—the books he sold—reflected his aesthetic sense. The text, illustrations, and borders on both visible pages were viewed by Morris as a whole; he sought balance and harmony among all the elements of a book. In his final work, where he discussed the activities of his press, Morris (1934) wrote:

> It was the essence of my undertaking to produce books which it would be a pleasure to look upon as pieces of printing and arrangement of type. Looking at my adventure from this point of view then, I found I had to consider chiefly the following things: the paper, the form of the type, the relative spacing of the letters, the words, and the lines; and lastly, the position of the printed matter on the page.

To achieve this vision of fine-art books, Morris employed Richard Cope's Albion Press, mentioned before. This handpress lowered the platen onto the form with a toggle action, instead of a screw, thereby producing a sharp image. And the paper used by the Kelmscott Press was handmade, containing the old-fashioned watermark and chain lines that automation had eliminated from nineteenth-century paper.

Working with engraver and type designer Emery Walker, and punch-cutter Edward Prince, Morris developed several new types for his book. The first was a Roman "Golden" type, based on Nicolaus Jenson's Venetian type of the sixteenth century. Two other types were the "Troy" and its smaller relative "Chaucer," both of which were derived from the tradition of Gothic types. Unlike the German fonts of the sixteenth century, however, Morris's types were aesthetically appealing and legible. Woodcuts in Morris's books were done by Sir Edward Burne-Jones, one of the most famous English illustrators of the period.

The Kelmscott Press printed for a brief period of time, 1891 through 1898, but in those seven years the Morris influence was felt throughout the publishing world. Typographers in Europe and America were drawn to the artistry of his books and the technical elements of his methods. Fifty-three books were printed—approximately 18,000 individual copies. Among these were *The Well at the World's End* and *The Earthly Paradise*, both authored by Morris himself. Ultimately, the Kelmscott Press inspired a generation of printers and artists to look beyond the technology of the present to locate and imitate aesthetic exemplars from the past. The "Arts and Crafts" movement (of which Frank Lloyd Wright was perhaps the most famous proponent), with its emphasis on high-quality materials, handcrafting, and an organic, naturalized design, was a direct result of Morris's artistic endeavors.

The technology of the book was truly in the midst of a revolution at the dawn of the twentieth century. The publishing industry, the instruments of book production, and the demands of readers were evolving in lockstep. It was an exciting time in the life of books.

6

The Future of Books: Twentieth Century and Beyond

In the nineteenth century, a series of dramatic changes swept the printing industry. Brought on by the innovations in automation, they altered the technology of the book as much as they did the fabric of society. Our seventeenth-century master, whose workshop was described at the beginning of Chapter 4, reflected the skill-set and craftsmanship of most printers from the time of Gutenberg up to the era of mechanization. With wooden presses, a small staff, and limited output, his shop was emblematic of book production in an era when every step—from typecasting to composition to impression—was done by hand.

As the previous chapter demonstrated, by 1850, automation had changed the landscape of the printing world. This era saw the rise of factories that dwarfed their print-shop predecessors, and mechanization leading to increasing specialization in the printing industry. By the mid-nineteenth century, the Imperial Government Printing Establishment in Vienna was operating forty-six cylinder presses and fifty iron handpresses, using over 3 million pounds of type, and employing nearly 900 workers (Gaskell 1995, 289). Small-scale artisanal shops either gave way to, or became, large-scale industrial operations. In 1817, James and John Harper established a small printing firm in New York. Within a decade, Harper & Brothers was the largest publisher in the United States, spawning the popular *Harper's Weekly*, a magazine with a circulation of over 200,000.

Growth in the printing industry would continue unabated through the twentieth century. By the year 2000, the information contained in one Sunday edition of the *New York Times* exceeded the total written information that a literate, eighteenth-century Englishman would likely have encountered in his entire lifetime. Mass production of information, and particularly, mass production of books, reached unimagined levels under the spur of technological innovation. In the twentieth century, the age of steam gave way to the age of electricity and, a mere seventy years later, to the age of computers. By the 1980s, it was possible to automate all aspects of book production without sacrificing quality. The computer age has profoundly affected the way books are designed, how they are printed, and the path through which they are marketed, distributed, and sold.

A niche market still remains for those interested in the craftsmanship and techniques of an earlier era, but the vast majority of printers, publishers, and booksellers have adjusted to these new technologies and to the increasingly specialized and fragmented nature of print readership.

BOOKS IN THE EARLY TWENTIETH CENTURY

As the previous chapter demonstrated, lithography and photography were among the most important technological innovations of the nineteenth century, and were critical to the development of modern techniques in book illustration. Photography was utilized by printers in several ways, most commonly by creating an image on a plate so that reproductions could easily be made. Photomechanical printing techniques, such as photogravure, developed in the nineteenth century, eliminated much of the artisanal skill that had gone into earlier books. But for the businessmen in this industry, these were clearly the methods of choice. At the turn of the century, a technique known as "photo-litho offset printing" was introduced, but to understand its value, the marriage of photography and lithography must first be considered.

Reproducing a photograph on a lithograph stone was the initial step, which required special preparation of the stone. First, the stone was roughened by machine, so that water would adhere to its surface, and then coated with photosensitive chemicals (called photoresists). A photographic negative was then placed on the stone and exposed to light, so that light passed through the clear parts of the negative, but did not penetrate the dark parts. The chemicals (resists) on the stone's surface that received the light hardened, while those beneath the dark parts of the negative did not. A greasy ink was then applied, as in lithography, which adhered to the hardened chemicals. Finally, when the entire stone was rinsed with water, ink was washed away from all areas except those spots that were beneath the clear parts of the photographic negative. The positive image had effectively been transferred to the stone and, following a few additional rinses, could be reproduced.

Photolithography was finally coupled with the offset printing process (described later) in 1904. The result was a revolution in printing and book production as profound as Gutenberg's in the fifteenth century. It is difficult to credit one person with developing the offset method. In America, several individuals developed the fundamental idea independently: the brothers Charles and Albert Harris, Baltimore printer Caspar Hermann, and New Jersey printer Ira Washington Rubel. Rubel, who owned a paper mill and lithography shop, came across his innovation entirely by accident. Through a sheetfeeding error, he managed to print a page not from the metal cylinder that contained the type, but rather, indirectly, from a rubber cylinder that had picked up the image. To Rubel's surprise, the page printed from the rubber was much clearer and sharper than those normally printed from the metal cylinder. He proceeded to develop this idea, and his offset rotary press was built two years later, in 1903, by the Potter Press Printing Company of New York. Almost immediately, Rubel's press was being used worldwide. The Harris brothers, for their part, started production of Harris offset presses, which became common industry-wide.

Fundamentally, offset printing involved two impressions, the first from an inked plate on a cylinder to an intermediate cylinder, and the second from the intermediate cylinder to paper. It is the transfer of the image through an intermediary that gives the method its name. Initially, this middle cylinder was covered in cardboard, but rubber was later found to provide a much better impression. Blanketed in rubber, the middle cylinder became known simply as the blanket cylinder. No longer did a platen push down on a bed of inked type or a paper-covered cylinder roll across the inked type bed. Offset surpassed these methods and quickly became the preferred printing technique for newspaper and book printers.

The details of offset printing are easily understood when the process is broken down. First, a plate cylinder was prepared for printing using the chemical (or electrochemical) techniques developed by earlier lithographers. Application of grease, for example, would allow ink to adhere to specific parts of the plate (i.e., where there was text). Soon after the introduction of offset, printers were able to purchase plates that were already prepared for printing, saving them considerable effort (Browne 1922, 24). Having been treated, the plate was wet down. The thin coating of water covered the entire plate, except where grease had been applied. Next, the plate was inked by rolling beneath the inking fountains. Small rollers ensured that the ink was evenly distributed over the surface of the plate. As it rotated, the

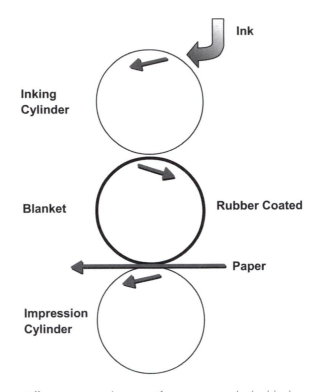

Offset printing technique. After receiving ink, the blanket cylinder transfers the image to the paper, which is supported by an impression cylinder.

ink clung to the greased parts of the plate and slid off the watery parts. Only occasionally would the ink break through a watery spot and leave an unintended mark. Such accidental blotches were known as "scum" and required the assistance of a pressman to clean the plate.

Having received the ink, the plate cylinder rotated against the blanket cylinder, transferring the image to its rubber surface. The blanket cylinder in turn revolved, transferring the image to paper. The impression cylinder situated below the paper acted as a platen, pressing upward against the blanket cylinder.

The advantages of this method were quickly realized by printers. First, impressions could be made at a rapid pace and printed pages needed no time to dry. They were immediately ready for use. Second, the method produced images and texts whose impressions were sharp and easily read. Third, the method was relatively inexpensive. The metal plates used—whether zinc or aluminum—were a mere $5, compared to the average lithographic stone, which was $100. They were also dependable, many capable of providing over 500,000 runs without deterioration. Finally, these plates could be easily and compactly stored over a period of time without cracking or losing their integrity, as lithographic stones often did. As for the rubber blanket, it too proved durable, capable of tens of thousands of impressions without wear.

Offset printing ushered in an age of high-quality impressions, the product of the rubber blanket, and it was soon advanced enough to allow for two-sided and multicolor printing. While single-color, one-sided presses involved three cylinders, offset perfecting presses required four cylinders: two plate cylinders and two blanket cylinders. No impression cylinder was needed because the blankets pressed against each other, so that both the front and back of the page were printed simultaneously. For two-color printing, seven cylinders were required. Paper would pass through the first system of three cylinders to receive the initial color, and then be transferred to a second, identical set of cylinders by a larger transfer cylinder. The transfer was necessary because there was no way that a single blanket could apply more than one color at a time.

The offset printing technique was utilized in the production of periodicals and books alike. But, as with all innovations in book manufacture, the technology did not eliminate the role of manual labor. On the contrary, as printing machines grew more complex, the role of the pressman became more critical—much more so than in the early days of the handpress, when brute strength was the only prerequisite. One writer commented expressly on the problems that arose when those unfamiliar with lithographic printing took command of a printing shop. Their expectations were unrealistic:

> Having no practical knowledge of lithography, they assumed that if a press was guaranteed to run at the rate of 5,000 [impressions] an hour, that would make 40,000 impressions a day's work. Of course, the lithographer who was familiar with flatbed and rotary presses knew there would be much time lost on the offset, due to stopping to work on the plate, to clean the blanket, and other causes. Hence he never made the mistake of figuring his press work on a basis of 5,000 an hour. (Browne 1922, 123)

His grievance continued, in a remark that reflects how commercial the printing industry had become:

> Some others have been disappointed because they put too much faith in the tales told them by the press salesman; as, for instance, that almost any bright young man in the pressroom could run the offset without any previous training, and that the less he knew about lithography the better he would get on.

To train these "bright young men," lithographers began organizing themselves in the nineteenth century. A trade journal *The National Lithographer*, was published in New York and circulated to lithographers throughout America. Numerous books were also published on the topic of offset printing. Their most significant organizing success, however, took place in 1915 when the Amalgamated Lithographers of America (ALA) was formed. This union represented workers in all areas of the lithographic industry, combining the former Stone and Plate Preparers Association with the Union of Litho Workmen. The ALA sought to protect the jobs of trained lithographers, preventing the above described scenario of untrained workers attempting to operate sophisticated machinery.

Offset printing brought speed and quality to book production. Hand-composition virtually died out, and the long-standing marriage between composition and impression ended in divorce. By 1950, most printers either purchased composed type from specialists or bought their own composing machines from major companies like Monotype. Lithographic plates came from lithography supply centers. It was a specialized and automated world.

During the Second World War, printing shops—like most industries—lost vital resources that were diverted to the war effort. But demand for cheap books only increased during the war, and when it was over, the printing industry thrived once again. To meet the growing demand from readers, printers worked on economical techniques for producing books, newspapers, magazines, and a host of other products. Among their developments was "aniline" printing, named after the quick-drying aniline oil used in the ink. Though the method was conceived and patented by a British printer in 1908, aniline printing did not become widely accepted in the industry until 1952, when it was renamed "flexographic" printing.

Essentially, flexographic printing is a form of relief printing from flexible stereo plates, thereby combining letterpress and rotogravure techniques of the previous century. Initially, these plates were made of rubber, but they were later replaced with UV-sensitive plates known as photopolymers. Using the special ink, flexographic plates transferred a very sharp image to a variety of substrates: paper, plastic bags, cartons, and cellophane wrap. Indeed, until the 1990s, flexographic printing was primarily used for printing packing materials. But today, flexography (or "flexo"—as it is sometimes called) is preferred over letterpress for printing paperbacks (Kilgour 1998, 141).

In addition to a variety of offset and flexographic printing techniques, the early twentieth century saw the introduction of an electrostatic printing process called "xerography." It is better known today in its applied form: the Xerox, or photocopy, machine. Students, teachers, and professionals from nearly every field frequently rely on these machines and their xerographic process, to make copies on a regular basis. Their ability to instantly reproduce the image and text on a sheet of paper, or in an entire book, has made xerographic machines an instrumental part of modern life.

Xerographic technology was first patented in 1937 by Chester Carlson, who initially called it "electrophotography." His inspiration was to combine two natural phenomena: the attraction of bodies that are oppositely charged, and the ability to make a nonconducting surface conducting by shining light on it. The atomic details of these actions are irrelevant here. Carlson understood them well, and he put the science into action by first giving a static charge to a plate. Critically, this plate was not naturally conductive, but became so when exposed to light. Carlson's next step was to project the image of a page onto the metal plate. As it was being projected, the light passed through part of the page where there was no text, hitting the plate. Where light hit the plate, the static charge drained away, but where the light hit text or image on the page, the light did not strike the plate. Thus, a charge remained on the plate precisely where text or image was on the original sheet.

This was the heart of Carlson's invention. He had only to dust the plate with small charged particles—a powdered toner. These charged particles were attracted to those areas on the plate where there was an opposite charge, the very spots where text and image had been projected. Finally, a piece of paper was pressed against the plate, the toner transferred from plate to paper, and a copy was made.

Carlson made his first successful photocopy in 1938, and his technique was purchased by the Haloid Company (later known as Xerox) in the 1950s. The potential of xerography was not immediately clear. However, once available to the public, its popularity was immense. The first Haloid machine, the #914, was sold to an office in 1960, and where Haloid marketing had calculated that offices might only make around 500 copies on a busy day, users were easily reproducing 2,000 to 3,000 pages per day from the start. The advantages of reproduction without having to wait were innumerable. From those needing a single document to those needing an entire book, the Xerox machine provided instant gratification. Later in the twentieth century, Carlson's Xerox would be adapted to create "on-demand" printing. But before turning to that revolution, we should look at the paperback revolution.

From Libraries to Paperbacks

In 1876, the United States Department of the Interior published a report detailing the history, condition, and management of numerous public libraries, principally along the East Coast. The late nineteenth and early twentieth century was a peak period for libraries, with the creation of the Dewey Decimal System, establishment of the American Library Association, and the founding of the *Library Journal*, a library publication still published today. The philanthropy of Andrew Carnegie was integral to the establishment of libraries across the nation. Between 1886 and 1919, Carnegie donated $40 million to build 1,679 libraries, many of those in small towns—such as Medford, Wisconsin, and Connellsville, Pennsylvania. The net result of this activity was an increasing interest in books among the reading public. With the greater access to books that libraries afforded, people from a variety of backgrounds, often those who never before would have considered themselves "readers," created a new market for publishers.

Publishers began to capitalize on the existence of this market, particularly in the United States and Britain, introducing cheap books to their customers. Such "dime-store novels" gave people the chance to own their favorites and to build a collection, eliminating the time constraints and other limitations associated with books borrowed from a library. Initially considered a second-rate product compared to their well-made hardback ancestors, paperbacks quickly emerged as a widely popular style of book.

Starting in 1837, Europeans enjoyed affordable reprints of the classics in the form of Tauchnitz editions. These were followed by the Everyman series, and then, in 1923, the Albatross editions entered the market, started by John Holroyd-Reece. All of these laid the groundwork for the paperback boom that would begin in the 1930s. No company better exemplifies this era than Penguin Books.

Founded in 1935 by Sir Allen Lane, the publishing house of Penguin Books was built on the notion that people had a right to purchase affordable literature. At the outset of Penguin's publishing enterprise, Lane commented on the paperback market in a manner that—in retrospect—rather understates the big business that paperback publishing would become.

> I would be the first to admit that there is no fortune in this series for anyone concerned, but if my premises are correct and these Penguins are the means of converting book-borrowers into book-buyers, I shall feel that I have perhaps added some small quota to the sum of those who during the last few years have worked for the popularization of the book-shop and the increased sale of books. (Lane 1935)

Lane could hardly have anticipated the boom in the paperback market that would follow Penguin's founding. Initially, the publisher issued reprints of ten classic works, including Ernest Hemingway's *A Farewell to Arms*, Susan Ertz's *Madame Claire*, and Agatha Christie's *The Mysterious Affair at Styles*. For each work, 20,000 copies were printed, and the publisher's success was nearly immediate.

Sales were facilitated by new marketing strategies. As a 1938 commentator on the book market said: "They are reaching this public through myriads of distribution channels, not merely through the bookshop proper, but through Woolworth's, the village shop, the small tobacconist, and the slot machine" (Hare 1995, 12). Combining style and substance with an affordable price and easy access, Penguin found a captive audience. The new age of paperbacks was officially under way.

A host of ideas and techniques in book production—going all the way back to Renaissance books—coalesced in these paperbacks. Their typefaces were based on seventeenth- and eighteenth-century models, but updated to reflect the modern sensibilities. The result was an aesthetically appealing type, capable of being mass-produced by Monotype machines, which reflected the kind of harmonious page William Morris had called for years earlier. In 1939, Penguin launched a subsidiary company, Pelican Books, which focused on the classics and nonfiction.

In the same year, the United States saw the founding of its first major paperback company. The June 19, 1939 *New York Times* ran an article headlined "OFFERS 25¢ BEST SELLERS."

> A publishing plan that will make available some of the leading best-selling books of recent years in unabridged form at 25 cents a copy is being launched today by Robert F. de Graff with the publication of the first ten titles of a series to be known as Pocket Books. . . . The new series will be sold in bookstores, drug and cigar stores and newsstands. The publisher hopes by distributing low-priced books through these mass market outlets to "open up new frontiers for the distribution of literature on a scale never before possible."

Pocket Books became nearly synonymous with paperback in the United States. The initial ten titles made available (at first only in New York City) quickly sold out, and by 1957, over 8 million copies of those initial ten books had been sold (Schick 1958, 129).

As the United States came closer to entering World War II, paperbacks continued to entertain a public wary of the rising global conflict. In 1941, Avon Pocket Books were introduced, offering mysteries and westerns that flew off store shelves. In 1943, servicemen were given a chance to enjoy the paperback revolution with the Armed Services Editions: small, horizontally printed books that could easily fit in a soldier's pocket. These books were only printed until 1947, but in less than five years, over 123 volumes were published. In 1949, Harlequin—the American publisher that would make the romance novel famous—made its debut, even though its first true romance would not appear for ten years.

By 1950, there were nearly $173 million in sales of paperbacks in the United States and Britain. But the milestone in paperback publishing was truly reached in 1960, when—for the first time—the sales of paperbacks exceeded those of hardback books.

In 1951, American novelist Harvey Swados commented on what has been termed the "paperback revolution." His doubts about the surge in the public's interest were hardly veiled.

> Whether this revolution in the reading habits of the American public means that we are being inundated by a flood of trash which will debase farther the popular taste, or that we shall now have available cheap editions of an ever-increasing list of classics, is a question of basic importance to our social and cultural development.

The revolution to which Swados referred is generally thought to have occurred between 1935 and 1960, and its catalyst was the production of cheap paperback editions by such publishers as Penguin, Pocket, and Avon.

Protecting Books

The twentieth century offered publishers automated composition, impression, and binding, making it a relatively simple thing to produce a book. Yet, authorial protection had not advanced much beyond the eighteenth-century laws—and even those were incongruent between different countries. The British Copyright Act of 1911, which extended to an author's heirs the control over his or her books for fifty years after their death, was an effort to remedy this problem. A caveat of the law, however, was that if twenty-five years had passed since an author's death, another party could legally reproduce the work in question, if the copyright holder received 20 percent of the royalties. While this discouraged some publishers, larger companies found it lucrative to go forward with the reprint before fifty years passed.

A secondary rule of the Copyright Act required that copies of books be deposited at major institutions and libraries, including the British Library, Cambridge University Library, and Trinity College Library (in Dublin).

LIFE AT THE END OF THE TWENTIETH CENTURY

In 1600, a writer who elected to print his work faced a lengthy and expensive process: locating a printer and a publisher, waiting for compositors, pressmen, editors, and binders to do their jobs, and then hoping that his book would earn him some reward—either patronage or monetary compensation—before pirated copies of his book appeared in the market. Progress in the world of publishing had been glacial. The overall process of having a book printed was hardly different in 1710 than it was in 1500. The range of choices of publisher, printer, and book style had significantly increased. There were some scant authorial rights recognized by the industry. But overall, not much had changed.

In the nineteenth century, though, books truly emerged as technological commodities. The Industrial Revolution, with its factories, steam power, and ubiquitous automation had ushered in the age of mass production. What an author now faced in getting a book to market was an industry, one that was fully automated. And as the power of steam, and later electricity, replaced manpower and craftsmanship in equal measure, these commodified books flooded the market at ever-cheaper prices, and they were purchased in ever-growing quantities.

Twentieth-century books were micro-technological innovations—the result of wholesale mechanization of printing. In a matter of a few years, paperbacks had inserted fiction and nonfiction alike into people's daily routines. But one fact hearkened back to printing's earliest days: even through the 1940s, books were ushered to the market by publishers who understood and dealt in the technology of printing.

This changed with the introduction of Desktop Publishing (DTP). The microprocessor brought book production into the realm of personal technology. DTP, as generally understood, involves any publication done at a desk, and as such can be traced back to the 1930s when typewriters were used to draft a book. But in the late twentieth century, desktop publishing came to be understood as:

> the preparation of typeset or near typeset documents on desktop computers (personal computers). All text composition, page makeup, manipulation of digitised graphics and integration of text and graphics are performed on desktop computers. ("Desktop Publishing" 1986)

DTP capitalizes on two key innovations of the 1980s: personal computers and laser printers. Used in tandem, these technologies allowed users to design their own books, replete with customized fonts, photographic images, and any desired layout. For large print runs or major publications, traditional printers and publishers remained the sensible choice, but for printing in small batches, desktop publishing transformed the home office into a personal printing shop.

In July 1985, the Aldus Company—named after the sixteenth-century Italian printer Aldus Manutius—introduced software called PageMaker. Designed by Paul Brainard, this program offered desktop publishers a set of tools previously available only to professional printers: page elements—whether text or images—that could be dragged and dropped into place, fonts that could be manipulated or created from scratch, and numerous tools for drawing. Moreover, images from other computer applications could be imported into PageMaker and set into a document. Printed on high-resolution printers, the result was a book (or other printed material) that appeared to be professionally typeset.

The result of this technology was twofold: First, it allowed individuals to produce brochures, magazines, and books without the aid of professionals. By 1990, customized books were easily printed with the sophisticated photocopying machines that, in a very primitive form, had started in the 1930s. Second, and just as importantly, DTP technology forced printers and publishers to adopt (and adapt) computers and related software for their own printing efforts. Books created with the aid of computers could not only be produced more cheaply and efficiently, but they also offered publishers unheard-of flexibility.

This technology evolved yet again when both the Xerox Company and Eastman Kodak developed electrostatic book-printing systems. This allowed for the reproduction of entire books at very little cost. Publishers who had books that were out of print could, upon request, print fifty or one hundred copies immediately, without having to produce an entire print run of thousands, using traditional printing equipment. An important concept underlying these machines is known as "on-demand" printing—the production of books (or other printed material) that is instant and not dictated by potential sales or estimated markets. Print runs could be as small as one.

BOOKS IN THE FUTURE: THE ELECTRONIC AGE

In his *Confessions*, St. Augustine described the reading habits of his mentor, St. Ambrose:

when he [Ambrose] read, his eyes scanned the page and his heart explored the meaning, but his voice was silent and his tongue was still . . . we found him reading in silence, for he never read aloud.

In the time of Augustine, around the fourth and fifth centuries C.E., books were traditionally read aloud, in part because they were so few in number. Reading audibly allowed the content of one book to be shared among many. Yet, the practice was continued even if one was reading in a room alone. It was therefore noteworthy to Augustine that Ambrose was processing the text without a sound.

Today, silent reading is as commonplace as books themselves, yet the tradition of being read to aloud—as children or adults—remains alive and well. Early recording media—wax cylinders and 78 rpm records—were too short to accept a book-length spoken-word piece, but with the first vinyl LP albums, authors found an appropriate medium on which to record. Thus, books from the Bible to the works of Shakespeare to the poetry of T. S. Eliot found their way into albums, which listeners could then enjoy in the comfort of their homes.

Cassette tapes, introduced in 1963, provided another medium on which to record the spoken word. However, the resulting "books on tape" enjoyed only modest popularity until the 1990s. Then, a combination of hectic lifestyles (which left little time for reading) and a significant car culture (commuters spending several hours a week getting to and from work) popularized the medium. Books on tape increased in sales by 75 percent between 1995 and 2000. Children's books, self-help works, romance novels, and mysteries have all enjoyed success as audiobooks. Travelers use the distraction to whittle away the miles, commuters escape the tedium of traffic jams, and those on the move enjoy their favorite books coming through their headphones. Moreover, textbooks can be put on tape and offered to students with disabilities, opening up educational opportunities to those who cannot read books in the traditional format.

As audio technologies merge with computers and the World Wide Web, books on tape are increasingly available as downloadable files. For a small fee, users can search a vast catalog of tens of thousands of unabridged books, download the audio file to their computer, transfer the file to whatever portable audio device they own, and enjoy the book virtually anywhere.

Electronic Books

e-book ★ *n. an electronic version of a printed book which can be read on a personal computer or handheld device designed specifically for this purpose.*

The above definition appears in the Oxford English Dictionary, a book that—like many others—is available in electronic form today. The page now before you, like the millions upon millions printed since the first Bible in Mainz, is an immutable thing. Once printed, its pages are permanent.

The most basic kinds of electronic books are presently available for download from a variety of private companies, universities, and public institutions. In the educational market, "Project Gutenberg" is notable for making 13,000 e-books available for free (nearly all are books out of copyright, and therefore in the public domain). Even more impressive is the University of Virginia's e-book library, which electronically sent 6.4 million e-books to readers between the years 2000 and 2002. That breaks down to 6.8 e-books per minute, every day, for two years!

In the commercial realm, businesses such as ebooks.com have made electronic books a big business, so much so that e-books are the fastest growing niche in today's highly competitive world of book publishing (Glazer 2004). The reader of an e-text simply buys the book online, the work having been typed into a computer or scanned into a file. Most services provide e-books in the commonly used Portable Document Format (pdf), making them readable on an array of electronic devices, from laptops to Personal Digital Assistants (PDAs). Even cell phones—with their relatively small screens—are used to read the downloaded text. Indeed, nearly 80 percent of e-books downloaded today are being read on some kind of handheld device.

According to studies, the number of e-books sold jumped to 71 percent from 2002 to 2003, when 1.4 million e-books were sold. Publishers estimate that $2.3 billion will be spent on e-books by the year 2005. This is still just a fraction of what is spent on traditional books, but with e-books' convenience and lower cost (most e-books are priced several dollars cheaper than their physical bookstore counterparts), there is reason to believe that their popularity will continue to grow. Major bookstores now offer e-books in every genre, from poetry to nonfiction to classics.

Academia, too, has moved in the direction of electronic books. Not only do technology-savvy students find it convenient to download books, but publishers are tuned in to the potential of turning textbooks into e-books. The dense science and humanities texts students have traditionally purchased can hardly be seen as efficient in the digital age. Thus, the highly competitive textbook market has led publishers to put textbooks in an accessible, user-friendly digital format. University students increasingly find that their reading can be done online. Coupled with "print-on-demand" technology, e-textbooks afford students a useable and economic alternative to traditional texts.

Still, many education professionals question whether e-learning can ever replace traditional methods. The medieval manuscript that university students studied in the year 1350 may have a timeless value. One marketing study determined that by 2005, electronic textbooks would account for only 14 percent of textbook sales. Even with projected increases over the next twenty years, it is hard to foresee a wholesale replacement of physical textbooks. For a time, e-books will have to serve as a complement to traditional texts still available in campus bookstores. The library, on the other hand, may eventually afford students access to all the e-books they need.

Public libraries are, in fact, increasingly moving toward e-books and electronic audiobooks for their collections. According to a *New York Times* report of December 9, 2004, the New York Public library has 3,000 titles in electronic form available for checkout, day and night. Within the first week that such e-books were made available, 1,000 digital books were downloaded (Gnatek 2004). Patrons of the library simply log on to the library's web site from any computer and type in their library card number. They then download the books they want to a laptop, PDA, cell phone, or desktop. Loans of e-books, like traditional books, are for a fixed period of time, so that at the due date the electronic file can no longer be read. There are no late fees because a reader is not capable of keeping an e-book beyond its due date. Only a limited number of e-copies are available for each book, due to licensing restrictions imposed by publishers. Thus, some popular e-books are put on patrons' waiting lists. When a copy is available for download, the patron receives an E-mail, logs on to the library, and downloads the book. Today's libraries, with their host of online offerings, can be patronized by people who never step foot on the premises or browse a card catalog. Yet, the technology of the e-book makes public libraries as viable as ever.

In an ironic twist, all of these e-books are reminiscent of the ancient Greek papyri in that readers find themselves scrolling through the document, which has no natural page breaks. However ancient in its style, scrolling provides modern readers with the ability to search a document for key words by using the computer's software. In an instant, an entire book can be scanned for a word or a phrase. In returning to its ancestral format, the e-book has provided readers with a dynamic set of tools they can use to interact with texts in new ways.

Finally, it is worth noting that e-books open the door to people who want to publish and market their work without finding a commercial publishing house. Today, anyone with a computer can write and then sell their e-book online, circumventing all the traditional publishing and printing mechanisms. For most authors, fortune does not lie at the end of this process, but the act of making a work public may be satisfaction enough.

E-technologies

Basic forms of e-books have become relatively commonplace, and the technology continues to be advanced. Today, entirely new conceptions of both paper and ink threaten to completely alter the way authors, printers, publishers, and readers think about printed material. In the near future, it seems probable that paper will become a relic of the past. Ink will cease to exist, and books will become ephemeral items, held in the hand at one minute, and erased entirely the next.

These notions all stem from the core idea of computerizing the very matter of the conventional book: the pages themselves. Numerous companies, discussed below, are in the process of testing components of truly electronic books and they promise a product that will usher in the most radical change in print culture since the fifteenth century. In the meantime, readers can still enjoy current forms of the downloadable e-book, read on a handheld device or a desktop computer.

The e-book revolution—as it can appropriately be termed—begins with electronic paper (e-paper) and electronic ink (e-ink). In these innovative media, the computer screen, with its convenient composition and erasure tools, meets the traditional flat, flexible, portable style of paper we are accustomed to.

The basic model of reusable e-paper incorporates the characteristics of normal paper: it is thin and light, it holds an image that can be viewed from many angles, and it is reasonably affordable. It also allows for the image on its surface to be erased—though unlike regular paper, one could erase and rewrite on e-paper thousands of times without compromising its quality. Another advantage of e-paper would be its shape and size: pages could range from the common $8\frac{1}{2} \times 11$ inches to larger poster-size sheets suitable for advertising in shop windows. And the appearance of either handwriting or type on the page would be sharp and clear, easily read, and—if need be—altered on the page.

Today, labs affiliated with several corporations, including the Xerox Corporation, have created an e-paper that differs from traditional wood pulp in every conceivable way. The Xerox Corporation uses what they call "Gyricon" technology (from the Greek word *gyro* meaning "rotate" and *icon*, meaning "image"), while the E Ink Corporation (founded in 1997) has developed "RadioPaper." The names are different but what these e-papers have in common is a thin, high-resolution display that allows images or text to appear, be erased, and change based on electronic input. A sheet of RadioPaper is no more than 0.3 mm thick (compared to traditional paper which is 1.2 mm thick) and can be rolled into a 4-mm cylinder, creating an electronic version of the ancient scrolls (Smalley 2003). Though the paper is literally an electronic screen, and the image is produced by e-ink, the appearance is that of traditional ink on paper.

To make this e-ink work within the paper, tiny beads—no wider than a human hair—are set inside a thin, transparent film of plastic (Ditlea 2001, 2). These beads can be thought of as spheres, each of which rotates inside its own pocket, or cavity. Half of each sphere is painted black, while the other half is white—though the colors may vary. Each bead is also polar, with a positive charge on one end and a negative charge on the other. This polarity allows them to be manipulated by an electrical charge, so that, in the presence of a current or electric field, some beads turn white-side up and others black-side up. Depending on the voltage pattern that is applied, different words, shapes, or images appear on the screen—the product of all the little beads arranging themselves in a particular pattern.

According to the E Ink Corporation, the advantages of electronic ink are threefold. First, only a very small amount of energy is required to create a sharp image with e-ink, and once the image is formed (and the beads are properly positioned) no additional energy is required to maintain it. This makes the technology highly efficient and—in the end—affordable. Second, e-ink is lightweight and can therefore be applied to an array of surfaces, from plastics to paper to metal. Finally, e-ink is highly flexible, so that when applied to a plastic, it can be bent around very small objects, such as a pencil.

When an image is produced, the effect is not unlike that of halftone in a newspaper, where a blend of small white and black dots produces shading and depth in an image. In this case, however, the shapes formed are controlled electronically. Using this schema, colors in images are also possible. Electric impulses could stimulate the emergence of yellows or reds in individual beads, each contained inside an entire color wheel that responds to different voltages (Ditlea 2001, 3).

This e-paper technique was pioneered by Nicholas Sheridon, who, in 2001, introduced a prototype for commercial use. On a thin screen, ostensibly the paper, words appeared, quite similar to those on a computer screen. But the so-called e-paper was still rigid, hardly like the paper commonly used for books. Moreover, the resolution of the image produced by e-ink paled in comparison to the quality of traditionally printed ink (100 dpi on e-paper versus 1,200 dpi on standard paper). The technology was promising, but still needed revision.

Scientists and engineers have continued to work on more flexible e-paper, with better resolution. Sheridon has conceptualized e-paper scrolls that would emerge from a cylinder, again hearkening back to the days of the papyrus scrolls. As the e-paper emerges, electronic impulses "print" onto the scroll (by manipulating beads embedded in the paper), yielding text that is either news, or a novel, or maps, depending on the needs of the reader. Because the paper is flexible and light, it is efficiently carried around. Moreover, it can be reused; the information on any sheet or scroll of e-paper is as erasable as a floppy disk. The days of wood pulp, it seems, are numbered.

Another innovative direction for e-books is the notion of an erasable book. Imagine that the book you are holding now contains electronic paper, and the words you are reading—while they appear to be typed—are actually created by electronic signals revolving little beads in the e-paper. Now imagine finishing this book and plugging it into your computer. Within seconds, the text is erased (electronically, all the beads are turned white-side up) and the new text—say, today's newspaper—appears on these pages. This is the erasable e-book, and it is not too far in the future. Joseph Jacobson, who develops e-book technologies at the Massachusetts Institute of Technology Media Lab, has envisioned what he calls the last book:

> several hundred bound pages of self-printing paper with a separate processor imprinted on each page and enough memory chips in the hardcover volume's spine to store the entire contents of the Library of Congress. (Ditlea 2001, 5)

One of the primary motivations for the development of e-books is the reduction of waste. Using traditional methods, each book that comes from a press requires trees, and lots of them. According to recent production statistics, the pulp from one tree will make nearly seventeen reams of paper, or 8,333 sheets. One ton of nonrecycled printing and office paper uses twenty-four trees. There is no doubt that the paper industry has a dramatic impact on the world's forests. E-paper, assuming it has no negative environmental impacts, is an environmentally sound alternative.

Conclusion

According to a report published by researchers at the University of California's School of Information Management and Systems, there were nearly 1 million new titles published worldwide in the year 2003 (141,901 in the United States). Nearly 2.75 billion books were sold around the globe. Of these, 1.62 billion books were purchased in the United States from a selection of over 2 million titles.

Given the tremendous numbers of books in the world, one can only

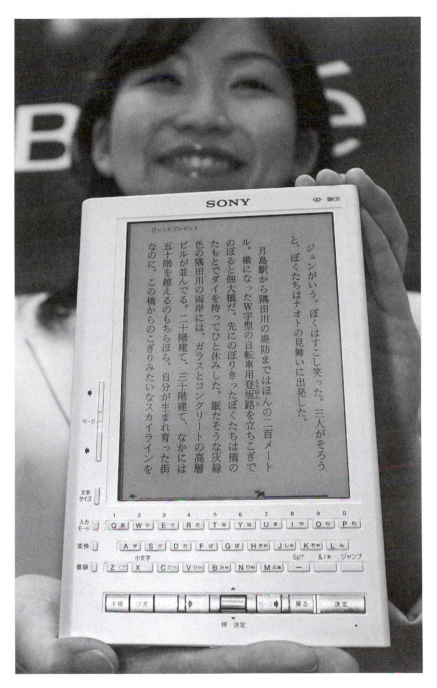

The future of books is electronic, according to many authors, publishers, and readers. Here, an image of an e-book. AFP/Getty Images.

speculate where book technology will go in the twenty-first century. To be sure, the future of electronic books is promising. Reusable e-paper and e-ink, coupled with microprocessing technology, could produce a single book that contains the potential to become any book in print. The life of the book could be consolidated in a single, electronic bundle, ink replaced by electrons, paper by flexible screens, and bindings by synthetic covers containing computer chips. But such notions remain, for the time being, largely the products of technological optimism.

However culture changes and however e-books develop, one can rest assured that fine-art books will remain—the products of wooden and iron handpresses that offer readers hand-composed types, hand-impressions, and hand-sewn bindings. As much as publishers anticipate the future of the book, there will always be printers who look to the book's past, in the hope of preserving the union of craftsmanship and technology that existed before and during the days of Gutenberg. Ultimately, the labor, equipment, and information that come together to record information result in the world's most critical technology: the book. It is a technology fundamental to understanding our past, and essential for moving into the future.

Glossary

Binding. The process of securing the leaves of a book together and fixing them to a cover. Bindings were originally sewn by hand in several styles. The covers attached to the bindings were often decorated with stamps, jewels, and other objects.

Block book. A book produced from wooden blocks—typically containing images alone—which are linked and then pressed onto parchment or paper. Block books, also called xylographic books, preceded books from moveable type.

Codex. A form of book that replaced the scrolls. Codices consisted of two manuscripts or tablets that were sewn together to make the shape of a book, often with a spine and a decorated cover. The codex was a common book format by the fifth century C.E.

Cover. The protective boards or paper placed on top of the pages of the book to preserve them. Covers were originally wooden boards, often wrapped in leather, but were later made of less durable, cheaper pasteboard.

Cylinder press. A flatbed press wherein a bed of type rolls beneath a cylinder that is wrapped with paper, thereby transferring the image from the inked type to the paper.

Diptych. A writing tablet common in antiquity, which consisted of two wooden boards, often hinged together with leather straps or metal clasps. The inner surfaces of the boards were coated in wax to receive an impression. The surface could later be erased and reused.

Engraving. Etching an image, often on a wood or metal surface. Engraving created a recessed—or intaglio—image, which was filled with ink and then transferred to paper.

Folio. A book size achieved by folding a piece of paper just one time, so that the leaves that result are half as big as the original sheet of paper.

Fourdrinier machine. A papermaking machine invented by Nicolas Louis Robert in 1798, which could make and feed a constant sheet of paper into a rotary press.

Gilding. The process of applying fine gold leaf to a page, the edges of a book, or the binding as a means of decoration.

Illumination. The often-colorful, painted images and ornamental letters in a manuscript or book, done by an illuminator. Typically considered a medieval art.

Incunables. From the Latin word for "cradle," incunables were the earliest printed books, produced before 1501.

Intaglio. An image made from a recessed design, which is engraved or etched into a block of wood or metal plate. The grooves created are filled with ink and the intaglio plate then pressed against paper, transferring the image. The opposite of intaglio is relief printing.

Linotype. A machine that automatically casts and sets a line of type according to the keyboard entries made by the operator. Invented by Ottmar Mergenthaler, it was in regular use by the late nineteenth century.

Lithography. Also known as planographic printing (neither relief nor intaglio), this process transfers an image from a stone or metal plate to paper. It takes advantage of the chemical properties of oil and water by allowing the oily image on the plate to receive ink, while the rest of the plate, which is washed in water, repels ink. Developed by Alois Senefelder, who built a lithographic press in 1817.

Monotype. A machine that, unlike Linotype, produces and casts individual pieces of type. Invented by Tolbert Lanston in the early 1890s.

Octavo. Book size that results from three folds of a piece of paper, producing sixteen individual pages, each leaf being one-eighth of the original size.

Offset. A method of printing that involves the transfer of an image from a plate to a rubber cylinder, and then to paper.

Paper. Introduced in China by Ts'ai Lun in 105 C.E. The earliest paper was made from the pulp of silk, but was subsequently made from cheaper cotton rags and, later, wood pulp.

Papyrus. Plants native to the Nile River region in Egypt whose pulp was used to create a writing surface. Papyrus sheets were glued together and rolled up in scrolls.

Parchment. Treated animal hides (often goat, sheep, or calf) that began to be used as a writing surface after papyrus became scarce. Originating in Pergamum in the second century B.C.E., parchment was the writing surface of choice until it was replaced largely by paper.

Press. A machine used to apply consistent pressure over a given area. In the fifteenth century, printing presses were built to transfer images from inked metal type to sheets of paper. These handpresses were replaced in the nineteenth century with automated presses.

Quarto. Book size achieved by folding a piece of paper two times, which results in eight smaller pages.

Recto. The right-hand page of a book when it is opened.

Relief. A method of printing from a raised image, often on blocks of wood. The extraneous wood is carved away, leaving the desired design standing out, ready to be inked.

Rotary press. A printing press that utilizes one or more rotating cylinders to transfer the image from type (or a plate) to paper.

Scroll. An early form of the book wherein the writing surface—typically papyrus— was rolled up for storage.

Textblock. The core of the book, including all the pages, which is put in between boards for binding.

Type. A rectangular block of metal or wood, which contains a figure or letter in relief and, once inked, is used to transfer the image to another surface. In the earliest days of print, type was cast in a mold, set by a composer, and then inked for printing.

Vellum. Material made from calfskin or sheepskin. Some scholars use the term vellum in reference to calfskin alone, reserving the term parchment for sheepskin, but such distinctions are uncommon in general literature.

Verso. The left-hand page of a book when it is opened.

Bibliography

Adams, Thomas F. *Typographia*. rev. ed. Philadelphia: L. Johnson & Co., 1861.

Alexander, J.J.G. *Medieval Illuminators and Their Methods of Work*. New Haven, CT: Yale University Press, 1992.

Allen, Edward Monington. *Harper's Dictionary of the Graphic Arts*. 1st ed. New York: Harper & Row, 1963.

Armstrong, Elizabeth, ed. *Before Copyright: The French Book-Privilege System, 1498–1526*. Cambridge Studies in Publishing and Printing History. Cambridge; New York: Cambridge University Press, 1990.

Berry, W. Turner, and Herbert Edmund Poole. *Annals of Printing: A Chronological Encyclopaedia from the Earliest Times to 1950*. Toronto, ON: University of Toronto Press, 1966.

Briggs, Asa. *Essays in the History of Publishing in Celebration of the 250th Anniversary of the House of Longman, 1724–1974*. London: Longman, 1974.

Browne, Warren Crittenden. *Offset Lithography: A Treatise on Printing in the Lithographic Manner from Metal Plates on Rubber Blanket Offset Presses*. New York: The National Lithographer, 1922.

Cambridge University Press. *The University Printing Houses at Cambridge from the Sixteenth to the Twentieth Century*. Cambridge: Cambridge University Press, 1962.

Carpenter, Kenneth E. *Books and Society in History: Papers of the Association of College and Research Libraries Rare Books and Manuscripts Preconference, 24–28 June, 1980, Boston, Massachusetts*. New York: R. R. Bowker Company, 1983.

Caruzzi, Richard Francis. *Offset Duplicator Techniques.* New York: H. L. Taylor, 1948.

Chappell, Warren, and Robert Bringhurst. *A Short History of the Printed Word.* 2nd ed. Point Roberts, WA: Hartley & Marks Publishers, 1999.

Clair, Colin. *Christopher Plantin.* London: Cassell, 1960.

Daly, Lowrie John. *The Medieval University, 1200–1400.* New York: Sheed and Ward, 1961.

Darnton, Robert. *The Business of Enlightenment: A Publishing History of the Encyclopédie.* Cambridge, MA: Belknap Press, 1979.

Davies, Martin. *Aldus Manutius: Printer and Publisher of Renaissance Venice.* Malibu, CA: J. Paul Getty Museum, 1995.

"Desktop Publishing." *Seybold Report on Desktop Publishing* 1, no. 1 (1986).

De Vinne, Theodore Low. *The Invention of Printing. A Collection of Facts and Opinions Descriptive of Early Prints and Playing Cards, the Blockbooks of the Fifteenth Century, the Legends of Lourens Janszoon Coster, of Haarlem, and the Work of John Gutenberg and His Associates.* Illustrated with Facsimiles of Early Types and Woodcuts. New York: F. Hart & Co., 1876.

Ditlea, Steve. "The Electronic Paper Chase." *Scientific American,* November 2001.

Drogin, Marc. *Medieval Calligraphy: Its History and Technique.* New York: Dover Publications, 1989.

Edwards, Mark U. *Printing, Propaganda, and Martin Luther.* Berkeley: University of California Press, 1994.

Eisenstein, Elizabeth L. *The Printing Revolution in Early Modern Europe.* Canto ed. Cambridge; New York: Cambridge University Press, 1993.

Febvre, Lucien Paul Victor, and Henri-Jean Martin. *The Coming of the Book: The Impact of Printing, 1450–1800.* Verso Classics, 10. Translated by David Gerard. London; New York: Verso, 1990.

Fletcher, H. George. *New Aldine Studies: Documentary Essays on the Life and Work of Aldus Manutius.* San Francisco: B. M. Rosenthal Inc., 1988.

Franklin, Benjamin. *Boston Printers, Publishers, and Booksellers, 1640–1800.* Boston: G. K. Hall, 1980.

Gartner, John. *Victorian Printing History.* Melbourne: Printing Industry Craftsmen of Australia, 1935.

Gaskell, Philip. *A New Introduction to Bibliography.* New Castle, DE: Oak Knoll Press, 1995. Distributed in the USA by Lyons & Burford.

Glazer, Sarah. "An Idea Whose Time Has Come." *New York Times,* December 5, 2004, national edition.

Gnatek, Tim. "Libraries Reach Out Online." *New York Times,* December 9, 2004, national edition.

Green, Samuel A. *Funeral Elegies: A Paper Presented at a Meeting of the Massachusetts Historical Society,* December 14, 1893. Boston: Massachusetts Historical Society, 1893.

Greenfield, Jane. *ABC of Bookbinding: An Unique Glossary with Over 700 Illustrations for Collectors & Librarians.* New Castle, DE: Oak Knoll Press, 1998.

Griffiths, Jeremy, and Derek Pearsall, eds. *Book Production and Publishing in Britain, 1375–1475.* Cambridge: Cambridge University Press, 1989.

Hare, Steve. *Penguin Portrait: Allen Lane and the Penguin Editors, 1935–1970.* London; New York: Penguin, 1995.

Hird, Kenneth F. *Offset Lithographic Technology.* South Holland, IL: Goodheart-Willcox, 1991.

Hoe, Robert. *A Short History of the Printing Press and of the Improvements in Printing Machinery from the Time of Gutenberg up to the Present Day.* New York: R. Hoe & Co., 1902.

Hunter, Dard. *Papermaking in Pioneer America.* Nineteenth-Century Book Arts and Printing History. Reprint. New York: Garland Publishing Inc., 1981.

Huss, Richard E. *The Printer's Composition Matrix: A History of Its Origin and Development.* Oak Knoll Series on the History of the Book. New Castle, DE: Oak Knoll Books, 1985.

Inwood, Stephen. *The Forgotten Genius.* San Francisco: MacAdam/Cage Publishing, 2004.

James, M. R. *The Ancient Libraries of Canterbury and Dover.* Cambridge: Cambridge University Press, 1903.

Jardine, Lisa. *Worldly Goods: A New History of the Renaissance.* New York: Nan A. Talese, 1996.

Jennet, Sean. *The Making of Books.* 4th ed. New York: Praeger, 1967.

Johns, Adrian. *The Nature of the Book: Print and Knowledge in the Making.* Chicago: University of Chicago Press, 1998.

Keynes, Geoffrey. *The Life of William Harvey.* Oxford: Clarendon Press, 1966.

Kilgour, Frederick G. *The Evolution of the Book.* New York: Oxford University Press, 1998.

King, Margaret L. *The Renaissance in Europe.* Boston: McGraw-Hill Higher Education, 2005.

König, Fredrich. "Letter to the Editor." *The Times,* December 8, 1814.

Kubler, George Adolf. *A New History of Stereotyping.* New York: J. J. Little & Ives Company, 1941.

Lane, Allen. "All About the Penguin Books," *The Bookseller,* May 22, 1935.

Lenhart, John M. *Pre-Reformation Printed Books: A Study in Statistical and Applied Bibliography.* New York: J. F. Wagner, 1935.

Lilly Library and International Printing Machinery and Allied Trades Exhibition. *Printing and the Mind of Man.* Bloomington: Lilly Library, Indiana University, 1973.

Lithographic Technical Foundation, Inc. *Platemaking for Offset Lithography: Deep-Etch.* New York: Lithographic Technical Foundation, Inc., 1946.

Lowry, Martin. *The World of Aldus Manutius: Business and Scholarship in Renaissance Venice.* Ithaca, NY: Cornell University Press, 1979.

Man, John. *The Gutenberg Revolution: The Story of a Genius and an Invention That Changed the World.* London: Review, 2002.

Martin, Henri-Jean. *The History and Power of Writing*. Chicago: University of Chicago Press, 1994.

Master Printers Association, Philadelphia [from old catalog]. *The Master Printer*. Philadelphia: The Master Printers Association, 1904.

McMurtrie, Douglas C. *A History of Printing in the United States; the Story of the Introduction of the Press and of Its History and Influence During the Pioneer Period in Each State of the Union*. New York: R. R. Bowker Company, 1936.

Morris, William. *A Note by William Morris on His Aims in Founding the Kelmscott Press*. With a short description of the press by Sydney Carlyle Cockerell. Large paper ed. London: London County Council Central School of Arts & Crafts, 1934.

Nutton, Vivian. *Historical Introduction to Andreas Vesalius's* De Humani Corporis Fabrica. Evanston: Northwestern University, Daniel Garrison and Malcolm Hast, 2003. Also available online at: http://vesalius.northwestern.edu/flash .html.

Oswald, John Clyde. *Printing in the Americas*. New York: Hacker Art Books, 1968.

Pollard, Alfred W. *An Essay on Colophons, with Specimens and Translations*. New York: B. Franklin, 1968.

R. Hoe & Company. *Catalogue of Printing Presses, and Printers' Materials*. Nineteenth-Century Book Arts and Printing History. New York: Garland Publishing Inc., 1980.

Redgrave, G. R. *Erhard Ratdolt and His Work at Venice, A Paper Read Before the Bibliographical Society November 20, 1893*. London: Printed for the Bibliographical Society, 1894.

Richardson, Brian. *Print Culture in Renaissance Italy: The Editor and the Vernacular Text, 1470–1600*. Cambridge Studies in Publishing and Printing History. Cambridge; New York: Cambridge University Press, 1994.

Roberts, Colin H., and T. C. Skeat. *The Birth of the Codex*. London: Oxford University Press, 1983.

Robinson, Pamela, and Rivkah Zim, eds. *Of the Making of Books: Medieval Manuscripts, Their Scribes and Readers. Essays Presented to M. B. Parkes*. Aldershot: Ashgate Publishing Co., 1997.

Roden, Robert F. *The Cambridge Press, 1638–1692: A History of the First Printing Press Established in English America, Together with a Bibliographical List of the Issues of the Press*. New York: B. Franklin, 1970.

Rostenberg, Leona, Madeleine B. Stern, and Terry Belanger. *Bookman's Quintet: Five Catalogues About Books: Bibliography, Printing History, Booksellers, Libraries, Presses, Collectors*. Newark, DE: Oak Knoll Books, 1980.

Savage, William. *Practical Hints on Decorative Printing: With Illustrations Engraved on Wood, and Printed in Colours at the Type Press*. Bruce Rogers, Frederic W. Goudy Collection (Library of Congress), and Pforzheimer Bruce Rogers Collection (Library of Congress). London: Messrs. Longman Hurst, 1823.

Schmeckebier, Laurence Frederick. *The Bureau of Engraving and Printing: Its History, Activities, and Organization*. Service Monographs of the United States Government; No. 56. New York: AMS Press, 1974.

Scholderer, Victor. *Johann Gutenberg: The Inventor of Printing*. 2nd ed. London: British Museum, 1970.

Schreuders, Piet. *The Book of Paperbacks: A Visual History of the Paperback*. London: Virgin Books, 1981.

Senefelder, Alois. *A Complete Course of Lithography*. New York: Da Capo Press, 1977.

_____. *The Invention of Lithography*. New York: The Fuchs & Lang Manufacturing Company, 1911.

Smalley, Eric. "Flexible Display Slims Down." *Technology Research News Magazine*, May 21/28, 2003. http://www.trnmag.com/Stories/2003/052103/Flexible%20_display_slims_down_052103.html.

Smeijers, Fred, and Robin Kinross. *Counterpunch: Making Type in the Sixteenth Century, Designing Typefaces Now*. London: Hyphen Press, 1996.

Smiles, Samuel. *Men of Invention and Industry*. New York: Harper & Brothers, 1885.

Smith, Dinitia. "Has History Been Too Generous To Gutenberg?" *New York Times*, January 27, 2001.

Sparling, Henry Halliday. *The Kelmscott Press and William Morris, Master-Craftsman*. London: MacMillan and Co., 1924.

Steinberg, S. H. *Five Hundred Years of Printing*. London: Faber and Faber, 1959.

Thomas, Isaiah. *The History of Printing in America, with a Biography of Printers, and an Account of Newspapers*. 2nd ed. Archaelogia Americana. Transactions and Collections of the American Antiquarian Society. Vols. 5–6. Albany, NY: J. Munsell, 1874.

Thorpe, James Ernest. *The Gutenberg Bible: Landmark in Learning*. 2nd ed. San Marino, CA: Huntington Library, 1999.

The Times. December 3, 1814.

The Times Publishing Company Ltd. *Printing in the Twentieth Century: A Survey. Reprinted from the Special Number of the Times, October 29, 1929*. London: *The Times* Publishing Company Ltd., 1930.

Vitale, Philip H. *Bibliography, Historical and Bibliothecal; A Handbook of Terms and Names*. Chicago: Loyola University Press, 1971.

Voet, Lâeon. *The Making of Books in the Renaissance as Told by the Archives of the Plantin-Moretus Museum*. New York: American Friends of the Plantin-Moretus Museum, 1966.

Wieruszowski, Helene. *The Medieval University; Masters, Students, Learning*. Princeton, NJ: Van Nostrand, 1966.

Winship, George Parker. *Gutenberg to Plantin; An Outline of the Early History of Printing*. New York: B. Franklin, 1968.

Winterich, John Tracy. *Early American Books & Printing*. Detroit, MI: Gale Research Co., 1974.

Wright, Esmond. *Franklin of Philadelphia*. Cambridge, MA: Belknap Press, 1986.

Index

About the Author

NICOLE HOWARD is Assistant Professor of History at California State University, Hayward.